FURIOUS FLOWER

Furious Flower

African American Poetry from the

Black Arts Movement to the Present

EDITED BY JOANNE V. GABBIN

University of Virginia Press   Charlottesville and London

University of Virginia Press
© 2004 by the Rector and Visitors of the University of Virginia
Printed in the United States of America on acid-free paper

First published 2004

Photographs © C. B. Claiborne, except p. 236 courtesy of Erica Bleeg

9 8 7 6 5 4 3 2 1

Library of Congress Cataloging-in-Publication Data

Furious flower : African American poetry from the Black arts movement to
the present / edited by Joanne V. Gabbin.
     p.   cm.
  ISBN 0-8139-2252-6 (cloth : alk. paper) – ISBN 0-8139-2253-4 (pbk. : alk.
paper)
    1. American poetry–African American authors. 2. American poetry–20th
century. 3. American poetry–21st century. 4. African Americans–Poetry.
I. Gabbin, Joanne V.
  PS591.N4 F87 2004
  811'.5080896073–dc21

2003012376

This book is published in association with the Center for American Places,
Santa Fe, New Mexico, and Harrisonburg, Virginia (www.americanplaces.org).

Dedicated to the memory of these poets whose spirit is evergreen

    Margaret Walker Alexander

    Gwendolyn Brooks

    June Jordan

    Raymond R. Patterson

    Sherley Anne Williams

And to the legacy of the Black Arts movement living in

    Amiri Baraka

    Sonia Sanchez

CONTENTS

PREFACE

*T*en years ago hundreds of poets, scholars, and poetry enthusi-asts gathered at the Furious Flower Poetry Conference on the campus of James Madison University. Transforming it into a liter-ary village, they came together to honor the elders Gwendolyn Brooks, Margaret Walker Alexander, Sam Allen, Raymond Patter-son, Mari Evans, Pinkie Gordon Lane, and Naomi Long Madgett; to explore African American poetry and the culture that enlivens it; and to pass that knowledge on to the next generation. This anthol-ogy is the result of their communal effort.

I am grateful to the poets who contributed their work to this anthology, and I deeply appreciate their keeping the faith during the long process from first submission to publication. I am particu-larly mindful of the encouragement of the late Gwendolyn Brooks, who called me on January 1, 2000, to wish me happy new year and thank me for my work. It was indeed a millennial moment, and one I will not forget because so much of what I had attempted to accom-plish in my career was acknowledged in her singular act of kindness and affection. Truly, I have been so fortunate in this literary life I have chosen because of mentors such as Gwendolyn Brooks, Mar-garet Walker Alexander, Sterling Brown, and George Kent. Their spirit encircles this project.

I want to thank my agents, George Thompson and Randy Jones, of the Center for American Places, who shepherded this book through several iterations and successfully placed it with the Uni-versity of Virginia Press. Their ardor for the collection never waned. I also want to thank Ellen Satrom and the entire staff at the Uni-versity of Virginia Press and especially the director, Penelope J. Kaiserlian, who took a personal interest in this book by making it one of her special projects.

The photographs by Claudius B. Claiborne are one of the hallmarks of this anthology. They give a retrospective of some of the conference participants and have the effect of freezing in the moment this historic event. I deeply appreciate his continuing role as official photographer for the Furious Flower Center. The intelligence and sensitivity he brings to this project are exceptional. I also thank Garrett McDowell for allowing me to include his poem "A Blooming in the Valley" in this anthology. I believe it captures the energy and magic that were palpable at Furious Flower.

A project of this size takes the cooperation of several people to make it happen. I want to thank my staff and the student assistants at the James Madison University Honors Program who provided much-needed clerical support. I am especially indebted to Renita Moore and Susan Schmeissing, who supplied invaluable administrative assistance with the preparation and organization of the manuscript.

After a decade of nurturing the phenomenon called Furious Flower, I have not lost my passion for documenting the growth and continuing vibrancy of African American poetry. For much of the energy that fuels this enthusiasm, I must thank my sister-friends in the Wintergreen Women Writers' Collective. They continue to provide me with examples of excellence and the literary courage to take on these projects. I am also grateful to my friends at Cave Canem, *Drumvoices Revue,* and the George Moses Horton Society, who help me to see the exciting future of African American poetry.

Finally, I am particularly fortunate to have grown up in a family of folk poets, storytellers, and singers. My brother, Leonard, and sister, Doris, looked forward to hearing the outrageous stories Mary Alice James, whom we affectionately call Aunt Mae, generously shared with us. I want to thank her for patiently waiting for me to finish all my projects so I could get to "the book" about her. As always, I am grateful for my daughter, Jessea Nayo, whose pride in me is inspiring and for my husband, Alexander, who never seems to tire of championing my success.

INTRODUCTION

*G*wendolyn Brooks's literary career serves as the inspiration, the touchstone, and the genesis of the idea for this anthology. Not only did lines from her poem "The Second Sermon on the Warpland" inspire the naming of the Furious Flower Poetry Conference held in 1994 on the campus of James Madison University, the poem has provided a striking metaphor for defining and understanding African American poetry.

> The time
> cracks into furious flower. Lifts its face
> all unashamed. And sways in wicked grace.

The metaphor Gwendolyn Brooks intended to describe a tumultuous time in America during the late 1960s serves well as a trope for African American poetry. We can read into these lines the urge toward a liberating identity crowded back in the language of Phillis Wheatley, or Countee Cullen's conundrum in "Yet Do I Marvel," or Amiri Baraka's call for a black poem that "All Black People Speak Silently or LOUD." We can read into these lines a literature that mirrors the beautiful and rageful struggle of African Americans toward expression.

Until her death in December 2000, Gwendolyn Brooks was the *furious flower,* whose heroic and eloquent portraiture of the lives of black people seeded and pollinated poetic expression throughout the second half of the twentieth century. Her winning the Pulitzer Prize in 1950 opened the gates for American writers of African descent to win other major literary awards. In 1968, when the Black Arts movement was gaining strength and followers, Brooks succeeded Carl Sandburg as poet laureate of Illinois. From this position she conducted writers' workshops for the Blackstone Rangers, inspired the activities of the Organization of Black American Culture, and became a major proponent of black publishers, namely Dudley Randall's Broadside Press and Haki R. Madhubuti's Third World Press. In the 1970s, when those in the feminist-womanist movement were looking for models, Brooks had a gallery of portraits of women that were anything but monolithic. Brooks became the twenty-ninth, and final, consultant in poetry to the Library of Congress in 1985. As the first black woman to be appointed to this position, she, in Sonia Sanchez's words, "demystified the Library." In the second part of Brooks's two-part autobiography, *Report from Part Two,* she delighted in the fact that all kinds of writers, once intimidated by its "cool magnificence, had felt free to come past marble and gold to see [her]" (84).

In 1994 the author of nearly thirty books, including poetry for adults and children, *Maud Martha* (her novel), and part one of her autobiography, Brooks was showered with numerous awards: Jefferson Lecturer from the National Endowment for the Humanities, National Book Award for Distinguished Contribution to American Letters, and the Furious Flower Lifetime Achievement Award. When more than thirteen hundred people gathered in Wilson Hall on the James Madison University campus to celebrate her distinguished career and her legendary generosity, two generations had grown up nurtured and nourished by her poetry. Michael S. Harper called Brooks a pioneer who had written beautiful sonnets and ballads and after carving out that territory had used the creative process to work against the tradition to create poems such as "A Bronzeville Mother Loiters in Mississippi. Meanwhile, a Mississippi Mother Burns Bacon." Dolores Kendrick, who sees poetry as a way to move people into a finer and truer recognition of themselves, said of Brooks's poems that they "Take you into yourself and bring you out whole again." Eugene B. Redmond acknowledges the continuing contribution of Gwendolyn Brooks and other poets who began writing in the 1940s and 1950s. He said in a conversation at the 1994 conference, "You can never fill their steps, you can never take their place, but you stand there because you want their light."

In significant ways, Brooks's fifty-five-year literary career has mirrored the commitment of contemporary African American poets who stand in the light. With a legacy of liberation dating back to the eighteenth century, African Americans have been creators of social values as they envisioned a world of justice and equality and eyed the prizes intended for every individual in America. They railed against the status quo and protested attitudes and institutions that stood to impede the human rights movement that changed the nature of American society. These poets have given voice to the civil rights struggles of the 1960s and 1970s and continue to cry in the wilderness of America today. Sometimes quietly and sometimes stridently, they have transformed society and reflected that transformation in their lines. These poets not only cultivated their agonizing and beautiful rage they also created their lines with intense beauty and truth in the service of universal humanism. They have imaged strokes of grace and heroism; they have celebrated the perennials: life, death, love, and music. History, myth, and prophecy flourish in their poems. And justice delicate as a lotus flower withers but for their constant tending.

With the lines from the poem "The Second Sermon on the Warpland," Gwendolyn Brooks thus created a metaphor that encapsulates the literary and cultural strivings of these poets as well as captures her own spirit. As the embodiment of the furious flower, Brooks was responsive to the dynamism, complexity, and richness that compose African American culture. Her fierce dedication to craft; her close examination of the stylistic, linguistic, and imagistic qualities of language; her reverence of the expressive originality of the black masses and their folk traditions; and her embracing the black aesthetic and a newly energized black audience make her poetic career a touchstone for the exploration of poetry during the second half of the twentieth century. As Maria K. Mootry suggests in the introduction to the book *A Life Distilled,* there is a dual commitment everywhere in Brooks's work: "In terms of art, she has never been wary of 'the fascination of what's difficult'; but in terms of social justice, she has always addressed a range of America's social problems. In short, at the nexus of Brooks's art lies a fundamental commitment to both the modernist aesthetics of art and the common ideal of social justice" (1).

From her earliest poems, Gwendolyn Brooks conveyed a spirit of militancy that she delivered sometimes with razor-sharp precision and at other times with indirection and irony. She exposed racism so virulent in the nation's armed services that the narrator in "Negro Hero" "had to kick their law into their teeth in order to save them." She laid bare the intricate horrors of lynching emanating from intimacy and innocence in "Ballad of Pearl May Lee" and "A Bronzeville Mother Loiters in Mississippi. Meanwhile, a Mississippi Mother Burns Bacon." She attacked the inanities of self-loathing and color consciousness in "Jessie Mitchell's Mother" and the insidious enslavement of Satin-Legs Smith whose "hats / Like bright umbrellas; and hysterical ties" are perverse antidotes for his oppression. It is not surprising then that these concerns merge in "The Second Sermon on the Warpland," a poem rooted in the black folk traditions we see in James Weldon Johnson's poetic sermons, Langston Hughes's urban blues and jazz riffs, and Sterling Brown's heroic folk characters animated by acts of struggle and survival.

Brooks made the poem an exhortation. Like the preacher who is a master of metaphor, she filled her call with a language that commands a response. It is a language stunning in its understatement and ellipses; it is a language that depends on the audience to perform the creative act.

> Whose half-black hands assemble oranges
> is tom-tom hearted
> (goes in bearing oranges and boom).
> And there are bells for orphans—
> and red and shriek and sheen.
> A garbageman is dignified
> as any diplomat.
> Big Bessie's feet hurt like nobody's business,
> but she stands—bigly—under the unruly scrutiny, stands in the
> wild weed.
>
> In the wild weed
> she is a citizen,
> and is a moment of highest quality; admirable.
>
> It is lonesome, yes. For we are the last of the loud.
> Nevertheless, live.
>
> Conduct your blooming in the noise and whip of the whirlwind.

It is significant that the poem is a sermon, for the sermon is at the heart of the sacred traditions of black people. The sermon demonstrates the striking communication of the preacher-poet, using language that is creative, experimental, prophetic, and lyrical. It carries the communal knowledge, like that from the lips of the ancient griot; the preacher dispenses the history, knowledge of rituals, and signs the community holds dear. It is part of a larger tradition that represents the source of much of Brooks's creativity. According to D. H. Melhem in *Heroism in the New Black Poetry*, "That center was, as Brooks put it in 'The Second Sermon on the Warpland,' 'tom-tom hearted,' African and African American, infused with the jazz and blues of Black music and with the sermonic power that varyingly touches all the poets in this study" (3). In "The Second Sermon on the Warpland" Brooks's message is redemptive. Her prophetic voice is urgent, unashamed, graceful, and radical. She tells us that, even amid the loneliness and the fear, we must live and "conduct [our] blooming in the noise and whip of the whirlwind."

In these "preachments" as Brooks was fond of calling them, she succeeds in defining an age of struggle and giving a prescription for health. Her poetic voice suggests a highly-charged time that calls upon the "tall-walkers," the "almost firm" to ride the whirlwind (*Report from Part One* 85).

In 1968, the year she published *In the Mecca* (the volume in which "The Second Sermon" appears), Gwendolyn Brooks reflected the maelstrom of social and political change that was reshaping the nation. The Civil Rights movement had scored some major victories. The Montgomery Bus Boycott, which brought Rosa Parks and Martin Luther King Jr. to national prominence, was the beginning of the end of discrimination in in-state transportation. The courage of the Freedom Riders opened interstate travel by bringing national attention to the violence against blacks. The Civil Rights Act of 1964 made discrimination illegal. The losses, however, were many. The senseless violence that had bloodied the history of black people in this country from the time of slavery was symbolized by the lynching of Emmett Till, a 14-year-old boy snared by Jim Crow in Mississippi. The assassination of NAACP organizer Medgar Evers in Jackson, Mississippi, and the bombing of the Sixteenth Street Baptist Church in Birmingham, where four girls were killed, would tragically foreshadow the assassination of Martin Luther King Jr. In *The Bean Eaters,* published in 1960, Brooks immortalized the tragic drama surrounding the death of Emmett Till, recorded in almost journalistic precision the violence encountered by blacks who dared to integrate a white neighborhood, and made us see the storm of hatred hurled at the children who integrated the high school in Little Rock, Arkansas. Later, in her poem "Malcolm X," Brooks captured the magnetism of the martyred leader with "hawk-man's eyes" who beguiled a black nation into being.

Malcolm's ideas provided the radical and philosophical framework for the Black Power and Black Arts movements. According to Larry Neal in *Visions of a Liberated Future* (1989), he "touched all aspects of contemporary black nationalism." In Brooks's words, "Original. / Ragged-round. / Rich-robust," Malcolm X sounded the tough urban street style and inspired a revolutionary world vision. With his image resonating in their consciousness, several of the voices in this anthology began writing in the 1960s and became moving spirits and visionaries of the Black Arts movement. Amiri Baraka absorbs the power of the spirit force that was Malcolm and saw the movement as a necessary means to create a literature that would fight for black people's liberation. This revolutionary fervor and commitment led Baraka, Larry Neal, and Askia M. Touré to create the Black Arts Repertory Theater School in Harlem and that led to Baraka's collaboration with Neal in publishing *Black Fire* (1968), the seminal anthology of the period.

Before 1968 Brooks had already experienced the palpable energy of a radical black activism that was present at the Second Fisk University Writers' Conference in April 1967. In *Report from Part One,* she recalls the incident:

> Coming from white white white South Dakota State College I arrived in Nashville, Tennessee, to give one more "reading." But blood-boiling surprise was in store for me. First, I was aware of a general energy, an electricity, in look, walk, speech, *gesture* of the young blackness I saw all about me. I had been "loved" at South Dakota State College. Here, I was coldly Respected. Here, the heroes included the novelist-director John Killens, editors David Llorens and Hoyt Fuller, playwright Ron Milner, historians John Henrik Clarke and Lerone Bennett (and even poor Lerone was taken to task, by irate members of a no-nonsense young audience, for affiliating himself with *Ebony Magazine,* considered at that time a traitor for allowing skin-bleach advertisements in its pages, and for over-featuring light-skinned women). Imamu Amiri Baraka, then "LeRoi Jones", was expected. He arrived in the middle of my offering, and when I called attention to his presence there was jubilee in Jubilee Hall. (84)

By Brooks's admission, she "had never been, before, in the general presence of such insouciance, such live firmness, such confident vigor, such determination to mold or carve something DEFINITE" (*Report from Part One* 85). In *A Life of Gwendolyn Brooks,* George Kent describes what she experienced as a "rebirth" at the Fisk University conference in 1967. The two historians opened the conference, which had as its theme "The Black Writer and Human

Rights." According to Kent, Clarke in a manner reminiscent of the southern folk preacher said, "It is singularly the mission of the black writer to tell his people what they have been, in order for them to understand what they are. And from this the people will clearly understand what they still must be" (197). After Clarke presented the history of blacks from the precolonial period through the abolitionist era to the age of protest, Bennett gave an impassioned call for a revolution that would remove "the last elements of white supremacy from the 'minds and hearts of black writers, themselves'" (198).

When Brooks got her opportunity to speak, she offered a cogent explanation of the dual role of poets:

> One of the more anxious wants of fundamental man is variety. The man from Africa is able to provide some because of the influence of an old music, an old and colorful land, because of the amazing crimes visited upon him, because of the rich quantity and quality of his response to those crimes. As I have said in Langston Hughes' *New Negro Poets USA,* in the works of Negro poets the reader will discover evidence of double dedication, hints that the artists have accepted a two-headed responsibility.
>
> Few have favored a track without flags or emblems of any racial kind, and even those few in their deliberate "renunciation" have offered race fed testimony of several sorts. I continue and violently to believe that, whatever the stimulating persuasion, poetry, not journalism, must be the result of involvement with emotions and idea and ink and paper. (Kent 199)

Gwendolyn Brooks was riding her own whirlwind of a generational shift from cultural integration into the American mainstream to the wild weed of the black aesthetic, a shift evident at the Fisk conference. She became aware of a growing urgency among the young black community being given voice by poets such as Baraka, Haki R. Madhubuti (Don L. Lee), Sonia Sanchez, Etheridge Knight, Walter Bradford, Nikki Giovanni, Askia M. Touré, Mari Evans, and Carolyn M. Rodgers. With their iconoclastic attacks on all aspects of white middle-class values, it is not surprising that they rejected unequivocally Western poetic conventions. Their poetic techniques emphasized free verse; typographical stylistics; irreverent, often scatological diction; and experimentation. In Sonia Sanchez's "For Sweet Honey in the Rock," she has reinvented this fervor as she extends her techniques: "i had come into the city carrying life in my eyes." In her "Under a Soprano Sky," we hear the lyricism of her sustained committed voice, often rendered in her deeply spiritual chanting-singing style. Eugene Redmond, Jayne Cortez, Kalamu ya Salaam, and Sterling D. Plumpp are representative of those poets in this anthology who incorporate rap, blues, jazz, and soul music in their poetry, making it move with the rhythm of contemporary beats. Nikki Giovanni, who achieved national popularity when she wedded her visionary, truth-telling poetry with gospel music, captures perhaps as well as anyone the sassiness and pride that are hallmarks of this generation in her classic poem "Nikki-Rosa." Haki Madhubuti sounds the notes in "The B Network" that remind us that many of his early poems established a cadence and a hip style so familiar to us now in hip-hop. With his explosive, annunciatory rap, he has been one of the most imitated poets among younger artists seeking to establish their own performance style. These poets expanded a world that had as its center the sound of African rhythms. It is alive with boldness and beauty, and old patterns are inverted.

Despite this shifting terrain, Gwendolyn Brooks's work is rooted firmly in a disciplined adherence to the essential task of transposing feelings and ideas into poetic language. Her voice provides the touchstones for excellence I have used to select and organize the poems in this anthology. Those that are most apparent include mastery of craft, exploration of forms found in a rich vernacular tradition, chronicling history through poetic portraiture, and implementing poetry as an agent of social change.

For Gwendolyn Brooks, mastery of the poetic form was of great importance. Critics, in assessing her poetry, have often used phrases such as "mastery of craft," "wordsmith," "word magician," and "technical wizardry." Her literary achievement is frequently symbolized by her history-making Pulitzer Prize. According to Haki Madhubuti in the preface of *Report from Part One,* "Her winning the Pulitzer Prize in 1950 is significant for a number of reasons other than her being the first person of African descent to do so. One unstated fact is obvious; *she was the best poet, black or white, writing in the country at the time.* Also in winning the Pulitzer she became internationally known and achieved a following from her own people whereas normally she would not have had access to them" (16). In this preface, Madhubuti sets up the tension between Brooks's "conditioned" accommodation to the European forms, definitions, allusions, and images and her deep involvement in the black urban life of Chicago and her growing awareness of her African self (14). Houston A. Baker makes note of this tension in *Singers of Daybreak* by stating that Brooks "writes tense, complex, rhythmic verse that contains the metaphysical complexities of John Donne and the word magic of Apollinaire, Pound, and Eliot." However, he explains that this modernist elegance is used "to explicate the condition of the black American trapped behind a veil that separates him from the white world. What one seems to have is 'white' style and 'black' content—two warring ideals in one dark body" (43). The issue becomes much more strained when the idea of universality enters the equation. Dan Jaffe, in "Gwendolyn Brooks: An Appreciation from the White Suburbs," writes, "The designation 'Black poetry' seems to me an unfortunate one to attach to her work. The label veils her considerable achievement" (Wright, *On Gwendolyn Brooks* 51). Later he makes the point more emphatically, "The label 'black poetry' cheapens the achievement of Gwendolyn Brooks. It recommends that race matters more than artistic vocation or individual voice" (53). It is clear that Jaffe could not see a connection among the designation "black poetry," the creative act of crafting poetry, and the imaginative genius needed to envision it.

Gwendolyn Brooks never experienced such confusion; she was a superb model for poets who pursued excellence in craft and registered the particular experience of living black in America in their poetry. Rita Dove, Yusef Komunyakaa, Lucille Clifton, Dolores Kendrick, Cornelius Eady, Toi Derricotte, Michael S. Harper, Pinkie Gordon Lane, and Naomi Long Madgett are a few of the poets whose poems have what Brooks would call the requisite mastery and mystery and whose poems she might describe as "shapely and persuasive excellences" (*Report from Part Two* 111). Rita Dove's poems from *On the Bus with Rosa Parks* skillfully marry history and portraiture. Cornelius Eady takes a page from national headlines with the Susan Smith murder case and gives poetic life to the myth of the black abductor in his poems from *Brutal Imagination.*

Gwendolyn Brooks, who achieved a similar feat with poems that tracked the trial of the murderers of Emmett Till, sowed seeds rich in portraiture. Gathering material from the vernacular tradition, she created memorable portraits in poems such as "DeWitt Williams on His Way to Lincoln Cemetery," "Mrs. Small," "Sadie and Maud," "Ballad of Pearl May Lee," "Queen of the Blues," "The Bean Eaters," and "The Life of Lincoln West." The vernacular tradition represents a matrix that is ceaselessly renewable in revealing the essence of African American culture. Stephen Henderson, in his now-classic book *Understanding the New Black Poetry* (1974), critically analyzes black poetry using music and speech referents to explain and appreciate its original and innovative forms. Henderson's work has allowed us to see that many African American poets have absorbed their themes, forms, and style from the oral culture and that the meaning of the poetry can be revealed by discussing it in terms of the theme, structure, and "saturation"—"fidelity to the observed or intuited truth of the Black experience in the United States" (10).

For a number of the poets in this anthology, music is an important referent and defining element in poetry, what Amiri Baraka calls "musicked speech." Their poems evidence a full absorption of musical forms, such as blues and jazz; call-and-response features; improvised lines; the tone, rhythm, and structure of folk forms; and the entire range of spoken virtuosity seen in the sermon, the rap, the dozens, signifyings, toasts, and folktales. Jayne Cortez has music leap off the page in "The Guitars I Used to Know." Her performance gains from verbal virtuosity that mimics the musicians' dexterity as they make their guitars moan, squeal, slide, jam, and slam. Sterling D. Plumpp in "Be-Bop" says,

> Be-bop is precise clumsiness.
> Awkward lyricism
> under a feather's control.

Or in "History, Hollers, and Horn," he defines this black music "as the entire geography of / my horn." While Carole B. Weatherford offers music that animates the portrait of a carnival snake charmer in "Queen Ijo's Blues," Joel Dias-Porter (DJ Renegade) in "Subterranean Night-Colored Magus" uses the riffs, syncopation, phrasing, and rhythms of jazz to deliver his portrait of Miles Davis:

> Miles could blue like Bird
>   freight like Trane
>   early like Bird
>   night like Trane
>   wing like Bird
>   rail like Trane
> Rumbling underground.

The indirection, understatement, and irony in which Brooks delighted as a part of her poetry resonate brilliantly in Nikki Giovanni's "Legacies" and "The Wrong Kitchen." The vernacular takes on a contemporary cool in Everett Hoagland's "Time Break." "The 'N' Word" is Mona Lisa Saloy's humorous deflation of the power of the term "nigger"; the poem reestablishes the tradition's insistence upon secular irreverence, originality, and liberated expression.

Vernacular black speech, music, storytelling, attitude, and style were afield as Gwendolyn Brooks grew her poems. She, like Sterling Brown, Margaret Walker Alexander, Margaret Burroughs, Robert Hayden, and Melvin B. Tolson, was a model for the younger poets as she absorbed the language, values, and culture in the loam of her poetic expression. However, no less essential was Brooks's ability to distill from a turbulent atmosphere a sensitive reading of her times. In an explication of stanza seven of her poem "Riders to the Blood-Red Wrath," she has one of the Freedom Riders say, in essence, that "the terrors, the sufferings of my past have honed me into a better human being. I grind my raw sufferings into a refined glass that enables me to get a good look at man's GENERAL inhumanity. Inhumanity is rampant everywhere" (*Report from Part One* 189).

Gwendolyn Brooks was clear about her purpose as a poet. Her poetry would be a lens through which we could see history and the gist of black humanity. Introducing the writer Kofi Awoonor at the Library of Congress on January 20, 1986, the first national Martin Luther King Jr. celebration day, Brooks singled out a truth that runs throughout black poetry:

All and any African writers–African French, African English, African American, African African–are unified by one powerful persuasion: the desire to avoid enslavement.

Out and promenading, *cleanly* promenading, or maybe *just under* a confusion of contradictory images, or maybe (sadly) DEEP down, or maybe braided *through* an offended consciousness–is the profound desire NOT to be a slave, NOT to be enslaved. (*Report from Part Two* 106)

For Brooks, warriors-poets such as Amiri Baraka, Sonia Sanchez, Haki R. Madhubuti, Nikki Giovanni, Askia M. Touré, and Eugene B. Redmond, whose poems are included in this anthology, bring more than technical brilliance to their writing. They convey a merciless vision that revolutionizes how we see language, experiment with substance and form, take poetic soundings off the page and into public places, and swell a necessary audience intent on transforming their commonwealth while demanding the illusive freedom.

The urge toward freedom is the subject of several poems featured in this anthology. In Elizabeth Alexander's poem "Passage," the tumultuous journey of Henry Porter, who shipped himself to the Philadelphian Mister William Still, comes alive in ways that history alone cannot achieve. It is replete with details that show the interior of the box as well as the interiority of Porter's mind.

> Freedom was near but un-
> imaginable. Anxiety roiled inside
> of him, a brew which corroded his stomach.

Samuel Allen in "The Apple Trees in Sussex" allows us to witness the blistering history of slavery, no less horrific for its irony and understatement.

> I did not climb the apple trees in Sussex
> or wait upon the queen in London town
> they courted me in sweltering Mississippi
> with birch and thong to bring the cotton down.

With the urge toward freedom always strong, those enslaved responded to their situation by escape or revolt, while others simply toughed it out. In "Nat Turner in the Clearing" Alvin Aubert remembers the slave revolt that wrote history in fire. "Ashes, Lord– / But warm still from the fire that cheered us." Nat Turner's thwarted stab for freedom is reduced to ashes, but there remains "The stillness of the word that persists quivering / And breath-moist on his tongue."

The windows through which we see the world of the past fill the lines of the poems in this anthology. Good poems, like good history, reclaim and honor the past. Jabari Asim, in a poem reminiscent of Brooks's "Negro Hero," writes of "1st Lt. Vernon J. Baker: Hero on the Hill." In this poem the heroism of Company C, 370th Infantry Regiment, 92nd Division, wrung from the most dire circumstances, is sung. Or perhaps the gestures of courage and grit are less obvious, as in Natasha Trethewey's poem "Drapery Factory, Gulfport, Mississippi, 1956":

> Her lips tighten speaking
> of quitting time when
> the colored women filed out slowly
> to have their purses checked,
> the insides laid open and exposed
> by the boss's hand.

But then she laughs
when she recalls the soiled Kotex
she saved, stuffed into a bag
in her purse, and Adam's look
on one white man's face, his hand
deep in knowledge.

Gwendolyn Brooks said in a 1967 interview that she got the material for much of her earlier and best-known poetry from witnessing "a good deal of life in the raw all about me" (*Report from Part One* 133). From her small second floor corner apartment at 623 East 63rd Street on Chicago's south side, she could look from one side to another and see life whole. Many poets in this anthology have a similar intimacy with their environments and the people who inhabit them. Opal Moore knows well the nooks and nuances of the sanctified black church. Her "Eulogy for Sister" exposes the egotistical, hypocritical and promiscuous minister-husband whose wife "would be God's / instrument" but rather dies in protest. In Adisa Vera Beatty's companion poems "Memorization" and "Geography," the speaker remembers the violent death of her father and makes of her body a road map so he can find her. Sharan Strange's poem "Offering" occupies a similar terrain:

Burning, it turns brown, the color
Of my father, whom I never pleased.
Too late, I stand at his bed, calling.
He is swathed in twisted sheets,
a heavy mummy that will not
eat or cry. Will he sleep when
a tall stranger comes to murder me?
Will I die this fourth time, or the next?

The vibrance, vigor, and technical integrity that Brooks admired in the work of two generations of poets whose poems appeared between 1960 and 1990, she also saw in a younger generation of poets who were moving on the scene during the waning years of the twentieth century. Their poems explore the interior lives of historical figures, expose emotions and experiences that illuminate public concerns, and revisit the ideals of the Black Arts movement in the language of a hip-hop nation. Many of these voices, such as Elizabeth Alexander, Jabari Asim, Thomas Sayers Ellis, Major Jackson,

John Keene, Sharan Strange, Natasha Trethewey, and Kevin Young, are represented in this anthology.

In the first years of this new century, African American poetry is again experiencing an expansive renewal. The emerging poets, some fresh from poetry incubators such as the Dark Room Collective and Cave Canem, find their voices. Their poetry is rich, organic, and authentic, affirming the regeneration of the black poetic tradition in America. This sense of renewal was dramatically evident at the watershed Furious Flower Poetry Conference in 1994 held on the campus of James Madison University in Virginia. Not since the historic black writers' conference at Fisk University in 1967 had so many writers gathered around one purpose. And never had a conference of this magnitude been devoted solely to African American poetry. The conference, dedicated to Gwendolyn Brooks, brought together three generations of poets. It was a singular idea—to come together to celebrate poetry, to celebrate the phenomenal development it had achieved over the past fifty years, and to celebrate a woman whose literary career had been emblematic of that development.

The last time I hosted Gwendolyn Brooks in Virginia was in October 1999. At the invitation of the University of Virginia Press and James Madison University, she had traveled from Chicago by train to Charlottesville to help launch my book *The Furious Flowering of African American Poetry*. After spending time with Gwendolyn at a lovely dinner party at the home of the director of the Press, the next morning I went to pick her up at the Omni Hotel in downtown Charlottesville. We were to travel over the mountain to Harrisonburg, sixty miles away, where she was scheduled to do a 10 o'clock reading at James Madison University. She was slow to come downstairs. I anxiously looked at my watch and was relieved to see that it was only 8:15 a.m. When Gwendolyn finally appeared, she was neatly dressed in a gray suit with a blue and gray plaid blouse. She wore a navy blue knit cap that encircled a leaner, yet still lively face. Her eyebrows arched to her question, "Do I look presentable?" "You look wonderful," I said, as I guided her to my little Nissan and apologized that she would have to stoop low to get into it.

On the way over Afton Mountain, I was relaxed; we were making good time. The fall foliage was at its peak of color. The morning fog, so common to the area, had already burned off to reveal an intensely blue sky. The conversation came easily. She told me about her morning ritual that involved taking the juice of a lemon and a lime with a little honey. She said it cleansed the system. She offered that it may help me with my own health regimen. We talked about Chicago, George Kent, the Chicago State University center in her name, her daughter, Nora, and her performance company called Chocolate Chips. I was so enjoying the conversation that I did not heed the flashing traffic sign that warned of a backup due to an accident near Exit 235 on Interstate 81. Before I could get off the highway we were in a 10-mile backup caused by an overturned tractor-trailer.

My composure gone, my mind racing to come up with a solution to get us to the campus on time, I fell silent. After inching along in traffic for more than forty-five minutes, we managed to get to a rest stop so I could make a call and let the waiting audience know that we would be delayed. I parked the car and hurried to the phone, leaving the door open. I was gone for several minutes as I made contingency plans. We would not make the 10 o'clock reading. When I returned to the car, Gwendolyn Brooks said, in a way that startled and saddened me, "Joanne, don't ever leave me again like that." For the first time during the entire visit, I was aware of an 82-year-old woman who felt very vulnerable. And I promised not to leave her.

When we finally arrived at JMU, the audience was waiting, and she gave a wonderful reading. We honored her with the dedication of the Furious Flower Center. She took several of us to lunch at a local restaurant that specializes in desserts. She insisted we try at least two. We then got in the car and traveled back to Charlottesville for a reading at the University of Virginia that night. When Gwendolyn Brooks finally mounted the stage to the thunderous applause of eight hundred people crowded in Old Cabell Hall, I watched her steps, slower and more tentative than I remembered, and thought about strength and vulnerability, about infirmity and firmness of spirit, about aging and ageless grace. She ended her reading with a poem that had become one of her favorite finale-poems, "Infirm":

Everybody here
is infirm.
Everybody here is infirm.
Oh. Mend me. Mend me. Lord

Today I
say to them
say to them

say to them, Lord:
look! I am beautiful, beautiful with
my wing that is wounded
my eye that is bonded
or my ear not funded
or my walk all a-wobble.
I'm enough to be beautiful.

You are
beautiful too.

Gwendolyn Brooks had filled us with the certainty that we were all beautiful. The magic of the evening continued until after midnight. She signed books and made a personal connection with every person waiting in a line that ran the length of the hall. Her magnanimous spirit of generosity and encouragement left a mark on all of us.

This anthology has Gwendolyn Brooks's mark on it. She was the inspiration to many who gathered in 1994 to celebrate her contribution to African American poetry; she provided the touchstones of excellence in poetry that characterize this anthology. She taught us that we are all vulnerable and strong, and if we are fortunate we can capture all of that in a poem.

FURIOUS FLOWER

*G*wendolyn Brooks

The Second Sermon on the Warpland

For Walter Bradford

1

This is the urgency: Live!
and have your blooming in the noise of the whirlwind.

2

Salve salvage in the spin.
Endorse the splendor splashes;
stylize the flawed utility;
prop a malign or failing light—
but know the whirlwind is our commonwealth.
Not the easy man, who rides above them all,
not the jumbo brigand,
not the pet bird of poets, that sweetest sonnet,
shall straddle the whirlwind.
Nevertheless, live.

3

All about are the cold places,
all about are the pushmen and jeopardy, theft—
all about are the stormers and scramblers but
what must our Season be, which starts from Fear?
Live and go out.
Define and
medicate the whirlwind.

4

The time
cracks into furious flower. Lifts its face
all unashamed. And sways in wicked grace.
Whose half-black hands assemble oranges
is tom-tom hearted
(goes in bearing oranges and boom).
And there are bells for orphans—
and red and shriek and sheen.
A garbageman is dignified
as any diplomat.

Big Bessie's feet hurt like nobody's business,
but she stands—bigly—under the unruly scrutiny, stands in the wild
  weed.

In the wild weed
she is a citizen,
and is a moment of highest quality; admirable.

It is lonesome, yes. For we are the last of the loud.
Nevertheless, live.

Conduct your blooming in the noise and whip of the whirlwind.

Winnie

Winnie Mandela, she
the non-fiction statement, the flight into resolving fiction,
vivid over the landscape, a sumptuous sun
for our warming, ointment at the gap of our wounding, sometimes
would like to be a little girl again.

Skipping down a country road, singing.

Or a young woman, flirting,
no cares beyond curl-braids and paint
and effecting no change, no swerve, no jangle.

But Winnie Mandela, she,
the She of our vision, the Code,
the articulate rehearsal, the founding mother, shall
direct our choir of makers and wide music.

Think of plants and beautiful weeds in the Wilderness.
They can't do a thing about it (they are told)
when trash is dumped at their roots.
Have no doubt they're indignant and daunted.
It is not what they wanted.

Winnie Mandela, she
is there to be vivid: there

to assemble, to conduct the old magic,
the frightened beauty, the trapped wild loveliness, the
crippled reach,
interrupted order, the stalled clarity.

Listen, my Sisters, Brothers, all ye
that dance on the brink of Blackness,
never falling in:
your vision your Code your Winnie is woman grown.

I Nelson the Mandela tell you so.

A Bronzeville Mother Loiters in Mississippi. Meanwhile, a Mississippi Mother Burns Bacon.

From the first it had been like a
Ballad. It had the beat inevitable. It had the blood.
A wildness cut up, and tied in little bunches,
Like the four-line stanzas of the ballads she had never quite
Understood—the ballads they had set her to, in school.

Herself: the milk-white maid, the "maid mild"
Of the ballad. Pursued
By the Dark Villain. Rescued by the Fine Prince.
The Happiness-Ever-After.
That was worth anything.
It was good to be a "maid mild."
That made the breath go fast.

Her bacon burned. She
Hastened to hide it in the step-on can, and
Drew more strips from the meat case. The eggs and sour-milk
    biscuits
Did well. She set out a jar
Of her new quince preserve.

. . . But there was a something about the matter of the Dark Villain.
He should have been older, perhaps.
The hacking down of a villain was more fun to think about

When his menace possessed undisputed breadth, undisputed
    height,
And a harsh kind of vice.
And best of all, when his history was cluttered
With the bones of many eaten knights and princesses.

The fun was disturbed, then all but nullified
When the Dark Villain was a blackish child
Of fourteen, with eyes still too young to be dirty,
And a mouth too young to have lost every reminder
Of its infant softness.

That boy must have been surprised! For
These were grown-ups. Grown-ups were supposed to be wise.
And the Fine Prince—and that other—so tall, so broad, so
Grown! Perhaps the boy had never guessed
That the trouble with grown-ups was that under the magnificent
    shell of adulthood, just under,
Waited the baby full of tantrums.

It occurred to her that there may have been something
Ridiculous in the picture of the Fine Prince
Rushing (rich with the breadth and height and
Mature solidness whose lack, in the Dark Villain, was impressing
    her,
Confronting her more and more as this first day after the trial
And acquittal wore on) rushing
With his heavy companion to hack down (unhorsed)
That little foe.
So much had happened, she could not remember now what that
    foe had done
Against her, or if anything had been done.
The one thing in the world that she did know and knew
With terrifying clarity was that her composition
Had disintegrated. That, although the pattern prevailed,
The breaks were everywhere. That she could think
Of no thread capable of the necessary
Sew-work.

She made the babies sit in their places at the table.
Then, before calling Him, she hurried

To the mirror with her comb and lipstick. It was necessary
To be more beautiful than ever.
The beautiful wife.
For sometimes she fancied he looked at her as though
Measuring her. As if he considered, Had she been worth It?

Had *she* been worth the blood, the cramped cries, the little stutter-
     ing bravado,
The gradual dulling of those Negro eyes,
The sudden, overwhelming *little-boyness* in that barn?
Whatever she might feel or half-feel, the lipstick necessity was
     something apart. He must never conclude
That she had not been worth It.

He sat down, the Fine Prince, and
Began buttering a biscuit. He looked at his hands.
He twisted in his chair, he scratched his nose.
He glanced again, almost secretly, at his hands.
More papers were in from the North, he mumbled. More
     meddling headlines.
With their pepper-words, "bestiality," and "barbarism," and
"Shocking."
The half-sneers he had mastered for the trial worked across
His sweet and pretty face.

What he'd like to do, he explained, was kill them all.
The time lost. The unwanted fame.
Still, it had been fun to show those intruders
A thing or two. To show that snappy-eyed mother,
That sassy, Northern, brown-black–

Nothing could stop Mississippi.

He knew that. Big Fella
Knew that.
And, what was so good, Mississippi knew that.
Nothing and nothing could stop Mississippi.
They could send in their petitions, and scar
Their newspapers with bleeding headlines. Their governors
Could appeal to Washington. . . .

"What I want," the older baby said, "is 'lasses on my jam."
Whereupon the younger baby
Picked up the molasses pitcher and threw
The molasses in his brother's face. Instantly
The Fine Prince leaned across the table and slapped
The small and smiling criminal.

She did not speak. When the Hand
Came down and away, and she could look at her child,
At her baby-child,
She could think only of blood.
Surely her baby's cheek
Had disappeared, and in its place, surely,
Hung a heaviness, a lengthening red, a red that had no end.
She shook her head. It was not true, of course.
It was not true at all. The
Child's face was as always, the
Color of the paste in her paste-jar.

She left the table, to the tune of the children's lamentations, which
     were shriller
Than ever. She
Looked out of a window. She said not a word. *That*
Was one of the new Somethings—
The fear,
Tying her as with iron.

Suddenly she felt his hands upon her. He had followed her
To the window. The children were whimpering now.
Such bits of tots. And she, their mother,
Could not protect them. She looked at her shoulders, still
Gripped in the claim of his hands. She tried, but could not resist
     the idea
That a red ooze was seeping, spreading darkly, thickly, slowly,
Over her white shoulders, her own shoulders,
And over all of Earth and Mars.

He whispered something to her, did the Fine Prince, something
About love, something about love and night and intention.

She heard no hoof-beat of the horse and saw no flash of the shin-
     ing steel.

He pulled her face around to meet
His, and there it was, close close,
For the first time in all those days and nights.
His mouth, wet and red,
So very, very, very red,
Closed over hers.

Then a sickness heaved within her. The courtroom Coca-Cola,
The courtroom beer and hate and sweat and drone,
Pushed like a wall against her. She wanted to bear it.
But his mouth would not go away and neither would the
Decapitated exclamation points in that Other Woman's eyes.

She did not scream.
She stood there.
But a hatred for him burst into glorious flower,
And its perfume enclasped them—big,
Bigger than all magnolias.

The last bleak news of the ballad.
The rest of the rugged music.
The last quatrain.

We Real Cool

The Pool Players.
Seven at the Golden Shovel.

We real cool. We
Left school. We

Lurk late. We
Strike straight. We

Sing sin. We
Thin gin. We

Jazz June. We
Die Soon.

The Near-Johannesburg Boy

In South Africa the Black
children ask each other:
"Have you been detained yet?
How many times have you been
detained?"

The herein boy does not live
in Johannesburg. He is not
allowed to live there. Perhaps
he lives in Soweto.

My way is from woe to wonder.
A Black boy near Johannesburg, hot
in the Hot Time.

Those people
do not like Black among the colors.
They do not like our
calling our country ours.
They say our country is not ours.

Those people.
Visiting the world as I visit the world.
Those people.
Their bleach is puckered and cruel.

It is work to speak of my Father. My Father.
His body was whole till they Stopped it.
Suddenly.
With a short shot.
But, before that, physically tall and among us,
he died every day. Every moment.
My Father. . . .
First was the crumpling.
No. First was the Fist-and-the-Fury.
Last was the crumpling. It is
a little used rag that is Under, it is not,
it is not my Father gone down.

About my Mother. My Mother
was this loud laugher
below the sunshine, below the starlight at festival.
My Mother is still this loud laugher!
Still moving straight in the Getting-It-Done (as she names it.)
Oh a strong eye is my Mother.
Except when it seems we are lax in our looking.

Well, enough of slump, enough of Old Story.
Like a clean spear of fire
I am moving. I am not still. I am ready
to be ready.
I shall flail
in the Hot Time.

Tonight I walk with
a hundred of playmates to where
the hurt Black of our skin is forbidden.
There, in the dark that is our dark, there,
a-pulse across earth that is our earth, there,
there exulting, there Exactly, there redeeming, there Roaring Up
(oh my Father)
we shall forge with the Fist-and-the-Fury:
we shall flail in the Hot Time:
we shall
we shall

Uncle Seagram

My uncle likes me too much.

I am five and a half years old, and in kindergarten.
In kindergarten everything is clean.

My uncle is six feet tall with seven bumps on his chin.
My uncle is six feet tall, and he stumbles.
He stumbles because of his Wonderful Medicine
packed in his pocket all times.

Family is ma and pa and my uncle,
three brothers, three sisters, and me.

Every night at my house we play checkers and dominoes.
My uncle sits *close*.
There aren't any shoes or socks on his feet.
Under the table a big toe tickles my ankle.
Under the oilcloth his thin knee beats into mine.
And mashes. And mashes.

When we look at TV
my uncle picks *me* to sit on his lap.
As I sit, he gets hard in the middle.
I squirm, but he keeps me, and kisses my ear.

I am not even a girl.

Once, when I went to the bathroom,
my uncle noticed, came in, shut the door,
put his long white tongue in my ear,
and whispered "We're Best Friends, and Family,
and we know how to keep Secrets."

My uncle likes me too much. I am worried.

I do not like my uncle anymore.

Samuel Allen

The Apple Trees in Sussex

> I did not climb the apple trees in Sussex
> or wait upon the queen in London town
> they courted me in sweltering Mississippi
> with birch and thong to bring the cotton down

For I have come
not to bring peace
but your heads in a block, my lovelies,
cried the captain
    of the slaver, standing
    out of Liverpool, plying
    between Guinea
    and the land of the glorious free
    the abiding place of the sullen, querulous slave;
and Montaigne reminds us that stout and aging ladies,
abandoned but not long forlorn,
plucked the eyes of their young male chattel
to shepherd a crouched submission
into their care.

Locked in the dungeon of those gutted years, doomed
    in time
pinned in the silent back rooms of unhindered desire,
to each his stock of dark rolling pride,
no seer to serve as overseer, who served as his own breeder
fertilizing the stunned flesh feeding the rows of cotton
deep in the blistering hell of Mississippi;
by the Delta they descended down
    into the pit
forsaken by Shango and Damballah, down
  to the fist and the terror, down
  to the whip and the whim
  to the blazing heat of the field by day
  and the raging lust of the big house by night and all pale
    and ravenous things.

> I did not climb the apple trees in Sussex
> I'll never hail the Queen in London town

I spent eternity in Mississippi
whose grace was death
        to bring the cotton down.

A Moment, Please

WHEN I GAZE AT THE SUN
                I walked to the subway booth
                for change for a dollar
AND KNOW THAT THIS GREAT EARTH
                Two adolescent girls stood there
                alive with eagerness to know
IS BUT A FRAGMENT FROM IT THROWN
                all in their new found world
                there was for them to know.
IN HEAT AND FLAME A BILLION YEARS AGO
                They looked at me and brightly asked
                "Are you Arabian?"
THAT THEN THIS WORLD WAS LIFELESS
                I smiled cautiously
                —for one grows cautious—
                shook my head
AS A BILLION HENCE,
                "Egyptian?"
IT SHALL AGAIN BE,
                Again I smiled and shook my head
                and walked away.
WHAT MOMENT IS IT THAT I AM BETRAYED,
                I've gone but seven paces now
OPPRESSED, CAST DOWN,
                and from behind comes swift the sneer
OR WARM WITH LOVE OR TRIUMPH?
                "Or Nigger?"

                A moment, please
WHAT IS IT THAT TO FURY I AM ROUSED?
                for still it takes a moment,
WHAT MEANING FOR ME
                now
IN THIS UNRESTED CLAN

```
            . . . I turned
THE DUPE OF SPACE
            and smiled
THE TOY OF TIME
            and shook my head.
```

The Lingering Doubt

The lingering doubt,
the nagging doubt—
perhaps they are right,
the races are hierarchical,
despite the rhetoric of equality,
notwithstanding all the shouting.

But I'd suggest we wait;
the evidence is not all in,
man's hegira not yet completed.
Agreed, it may appear that a race
is genetically defective
by nature oppressive
an excess of yang in the blood;
it is clear
wherever he has gone
chaos and destruction ensue,
the smashing of cultures,
the shrewd sequence of priest, soldier, merchant
pirate, slaver, buccaneer
butcher of world civilizations—
but before we close the ledger
and conclude his moral unfitness forever,
let us seek rather to contemplate him charitably
to view him as a man
    among his fellow men
endowed with the full potential of all men
and able to shed those traits
    which so mar his bloody history.
Let us hope
he may yet be raised

in the aspect of eternity,
in the sight of a generous God
to moral worthiness
or yet—and it can only finally be so—
raise himself.

To Satch

Sometimes I feel like I will *never* stop
Just go on forever
Till one fine mornin
I'm gonna reach up and grab me a handfulla stars
Swing out my long lean leg
And whip three hot strikes burnin down the heavens
And look over at God and say
How about that!

*A*dam David Miller

My Trip

My trip begins
in a slender house
in a thick wood.

Weak light
guides the midwife
as she pulls me out.

Grandma Ozelia shouts,
"Praise the Lord!"

Then grandma's farm
its cows, pigs, the mule,
and my rabbit
suffocates
under a pile
of barnyard lumber.

Aunts and uncles
who tend me
when my mother
has to leave
my father,
and who are soon to join
the '20s Migration
North.

"Snake holes"
to stand over,
my first punishment
for theft, of my
youngest uncle's
elderberry wine.

Then the small town,
many houses, each
we live in for
far too short a time.

My sisters' books
from school
amo, amas, amat,
they practice
their Latin lessons
on four-year old me.

The pre-Depression
store we own
one winter;
my step-father
gives credit

to his friends
despite my mother's
warning, then
sawmill whistle
lays them all off.

On railroad tracks
kerosene holder
for kitchen stove
drops and smashes
while moving
to cheaper house;
no money
to replace.

Barefoot to negro school,
white children torment us
as we pass their place;
never to use public
library or any
tax-supported
leisure space;
bright enough
to sense a wrong.

Working from age nine
like my buddies
at odd jobs
after school, week-ends;

Eleven-year old
favorite sister dies;
why, why, why?

Good times, eating
hot candied yams,
butter dripping,
stone-ground
whole wheat rolls
from government issue
flour, a puppy
one whole summer long.

Reading books,
winning a bible verse
contest at ten.

Mulatto-run House
for white men
down the street
where I make
good money
shining shoes;
madam mistress
to police chief.

Falling from
every ladder,
fence or tree
I climb, yet
forever climbing.

"That boy live
to see twelve
will be a miracle,"
my mother swears.

I do live
and in my most
Jesus voice
announce:

"I must be about
my Father's business,
now that I'm twelve."

"You better sit down here
and eat your dinner
before it gets cold.
Father's business
your big foot,"
my mother scoffs.

A prophet is never
received well
in his own country,
I remind her.

Like the Rock of Ages
She can not
be moved.

Forever Afternoon

> What is death to the caterpillar
> we call a butterfly
> —Anon.

Ladder of success is an image I abhor.
I prefer the double helix, intertwining spirals.

My spirit does not wear down
or wear out, like a car or a shoe.

While my body wanes, waxes my spirit brighter.

I am in eternal metamorphosis.
Constantly consumed,
I consume myself.

Life has no stages; the word resolution
lies; life has questions, connections.

Life is a wheel of fortune, my life
a gift to be passed around the wheel.

Do we ask where does the caterpillar
go when it becomes a butterfly?

The caterpillar does not go, it becomes.

Spirit of caterpillar lives in butterfly,
same heart, beating stronger.

Song of the Wheel

To Trudie Palm

Your wheel sings, Potter,
circles within circles, meditation time.

Body anchored, your mind soars;
Strapped to the wheel, you become a bird.

Touch is your talisman, clay the batter
where you mold rituals of stone.

Print leaves, grasses in clay, tracks
from the earth, marks of faith.

You thrill to the pull of the wheel,
rounds enchant you. Search the soil
as savior, the magic of clay.

At the edge of the song,
you search for friendly forms.

In exaltation, from them you learn
to water the spirit of dust.

Pinkie Gordon Lane

Girl at the Window

She sits there,
hand on cheek, head
turned towards the open window
where shadows pulsate
like quivering beasts.

Summer and autumn
contend in blue skies
and spiraling air—
ghosts and green light
a mere breath touching.

A golden animal streaks
across space
and lavender hills outline
the rim.

Will they tell
the level of seasons?
Will they fly home
to the sky?

> Her skin is copper-toned
> and eyes the nests
> of birds. She
> dreams of Nairobi
> and wildebeests
>
> the equator a blue line
> slung in midair.

Lyric: I Am Looking at Music

It is the color of light,
the shape of sound
high in the evergreens.

It lies suspended in hills,
a blue line in a red
sky.

I am looking at sound.
I am hearing the brightness
of high bluffs and almond
trees. I am
tasting the wilderness of lakes,
rivers, and streams
caught in an angle
of song.

I am remembering water
that glows in the dawn,
motion tumbled
in earth, life hidden in mounds.

I am dancing a bright
beam of light.

I am remembering love.

Children

In the mid-dark if early night
we talked about how babies
were made, or came into the world.
We went to the barn
and shot pigeons with our
slingshots, watching them flutter
like frightened children
and drop like half-ripe apples
in a windstorm.

The really crowning times
came when we tormented
Aaron, shutting him out
of the lockets of our love

and watched him squirm
like a dismembered June bug–
yearning for us to let him in
while we turned the key
and slid the latch
that forever sealed him out.

His revenge was perfect:
he turned his ass
to family
stole tires off cars
spit on our proud name
and embraced the
penitentiary . . .
spilling his own light
like a plunging star . . .

Naomi Long Madgett

Reluctant Light

In memory of Maude Salena Hilton Long

Mother, I didn't mean to slight you but
it wasn't you that I adored.
You hid your energy in shadows
and I was dazzled by the sun.

I idolized the one whose voice soared to prophetic heights,
whose words rejuvenated epics of the ages. Some fine June
    Sundays,
slender and magnificent in morning coat, he would electrify the
    pulpit
with eloquent pronouncements of doom and glory so divine
the very gates of heaven seemed to part, bathing the atmosphere
    in crystal light.
Seeking his favor, I rehearsed raising my hand like his in
    benediction,
earning the childhood name of Preacher, shortened in time to
    Preat.

You gave us daily sustenance but there was never
a choir's fanfare or the soulbeat of the mighty to grant applause.
You baked the bread for which we seldom thanked you,
canned pears for winter and mended Depression-weary clothes,
scrubbing sheets on a washboard, humming hymns to lift your
    sagging spirit,
and cultivating beauty in endless flower pots.
The summer when he toured the streets of ancient Palestine and
    Rome,
you consoled yourself by painting pictures of the Appian Way
using the kitchen table for an easel.

You coached me in my homework, rejoiced
in my small triumphs and prepared me to confront the enemy,
tapping your umbrella against my fifth grade teacher's desk
to punctuate your firm demand for justice. I didn't recognize
your subtle power that led me through blind, airless caves,
your quiet elegance that taught me dignity—nor could I know
the wind that bore *him* high into the sunlight

emanated from your breath. I didn't want your journey,
rebelled against your sober ways.

But I have walked through my own shadows and, like you,
transcended glitter. I have learned
that I am source and substance of a different kind of light.

Now when they say I look like you and tell me
that I have deepened to your wisdom, softened
to your easy grace, I claim my place with honor
in that court of dusky queens whose strength and beauty
invented suns that others only borrow. And Mother,
I am glad to be your child.

The Last Happy Day

In memory of Alfred O. and Irene Hunter Williams

JULY PHOTOGRAPHS

1. The Godchild and Her Daughter
   The prepubescent girl circles her mother's waist
   with spindly arms growing too fast for her body.

   Behind them a jovial sun dazzles the depths of green
   and scarlet in leaves and blood-ripe roses.

   Just out of sight, the old pair
   whose love is deep-rooted as ancient olive trees
   smile at their little girl
   now grown to woman hood and mother of the child.

   Nobody asks, "Where will tomorrow take us?" Enough
   to be together here encircled by a wreath of sunlit love.

   We too have grown gnarled together.
   We count the common rings
   in the trees we have become.

Our roots sink into deep soil
and our bark is impervious
to wind and weather.

2. The Man
Cameras catch the sunlight's vigor
dancing in his eyes. In the velvet dark
his face turns like a sunflower to the brightness
he can no longer see. His fingers remember
the soil's rich balm, the profusion of petals-
daylilies and roses-splashed with gold.
His laughter is a deep-throated bird among them.

Suddenly a shadow falls
across his brow, his hair's
cool silver the one
remaining light.

Nine days to doom,
nine days to paradise.
One perfect hour before
the daylight dies.

SEQUEL: THE WOMAN

Summer does not dissolve
to autumn, then winter
but jolts and quakes
as the widow's tears
gush in vain to soothe and mend
the broken earth.

DECEMBER FINALE

1. And then,
as though his spirit called her
(but not so full of terror
and surprise!)

as though
he spoke her name

(but never wishing her goodness
to deliver her to evil!)

she was wrenched away.

2. Morning and conversation with a friend,
   interrupted by insistent jangling at the door.
   "The boy is back, says he dropped the lunch
   I packed for him. Claims somebody in a car
   was chasing him. I'd better hang up now.
   Talk to you later."

                Stealthy fingers rifle
the open purse. How to confront him, how
reprimand the audacity of one so frequently
befriended? Suddenly, raw energy unleashed,
animal eyes ferocious. Phone yanked from mooring
by hands no longer boy's but brutal hammers pounding,
bashing. A single scream for him who can
no longer hear, whose blind eyes, even if he could
be with her, would leave him helpless to defend.
Then the length of rope produced from nowhere,
whipped into place, stretched taut against tender
flesh, vulnerable cartilage. The mouth open
gasping for air, the bulging eyes pleading until
the kindness of eternal dark engulfs her.

        By what shall we remember you? Not
        the eggs spilled on the kitchen floor
        or the now rotting meat intended to relieve
        his savage hunger. Not your stifled wail
        beating forever against our throats, or the sound
        of your head bumping down the basement steps—
        the congealed blood under the pulp of your face—
        the broomstick left protruding from your anus.

        Ironic now the photographs in summer's
        idyllic garden on the last happy day
        we shared. But "nothing worth keeping
        is ever lost in this world." Even in *this* world
        may the love-deep roots of trees

conquer evil's senseless blight
and the perennial flowering of your memory
sustain us through whatever winter weather
we still may know.

Packrat

My trouble is
I always try to save
everything

old clocks and calendars
expired words buried
in open graves

But hoarded grains of sand
keep shifting as rivers
redefine boundaries and seasons

Lengths of old string
rolled into neat balls
neither measure nor bind

nor do shelves laden with rancid sweets
preserve
what ants continually nibble away

Love should be eaten
while it is ripe
and then the pits discarded

Lord give me at last
one cracked bowl holding
absolutely nothing

*D*olores Kendrick

For Gwendolyn Brooks: As I Civilize a Space

> . . . Rise bloody, **maybe** not too late
> For having first to civilize a space
> Wherein to play your violin with grace.
> –from *The Womanhood*

My violin is out of shape. The tunes don't come forth well.
no sweetness or sourness, no extremes. Something in the
netherzone I think, where things tweak or lie still.

The strings subdue the sound,
all of her is sound,
the primordial sound that converts
what is lonely to love,

that sees a grace in bloom
before the shadows are conceived.

This woman.

My fears are extensive, my demons dangling,
and my bunions ache. But once I knew a stranger,
lashed him to my soul when his horrors hit him
took him over the high road because he was old
and lonely and needed a terror to live with.

She looks demons in the face,
diffuses them with a smile,
springs you to her soul and carries
you over the bridge of the high road
on her back, if she must:

This woman.

I have known monsters in my sleep
prowling around in the bedding of my dreams.
Some call them nightmares,
but I dare not nightmare now.
Something has broken the spell.

And she, like morning light, easing
its way into syllables of light,
leaving the leftovers for dampened things to eat.

I am leaving Chicago on a DC-10.
I have a fear of this carrier,
too many things go wrong.
I would rather fly crow, I say.

But today is your eightieth birthday.
And I am here. What sends me forth
is unimportant. Love casts out fear.
For now I can share this civilized space
which I have learned to create
with the one who sprang the soft music
within me, called it forth, blessed it.

This act of love this gift this transcendent talent this Woman.

Not even the crow can carry there.
The ascent to eighty in this woman knows no altitude.

Where the Grieved Ones Sat

Seeing these church pews up in the Choir,
tense, swollen, mahogany mattered,
whispering their memories like songs
spilling from the voices surrounding them,
the spirituals of season survived
and Bachnerian Black ensembles of pain
gone holy.

She stops,
senses, watches
the ghosts
of the old ones
the elders
who sat there once,
long ago in silence,

their apparitions
of energy singing singing
a capella, a grief
of giving long after
their graves
beat into the hollows
of their last and final
remembrances.

There is a Power, here, she thinks,
they were assembled here because they were Black
because a white thing could not live
with their indulgent Blackness, because they were
empowered to hear for the white ones who sat there.
Only the white ones didn't know it.
Empowerment came afterward.

Now she hears their music,
their grieving souls
like sentinels crying out
over the body of the church
that lies in state: not dead,
not unforgiven,
just formulated in its oblivion
of death, asking alms of reconciliation.
And the church each Sunday is in mourning,
which of itself is celebration.

I celebrate you, she sings while the choir puts
adagios together. Sing in me and I will sing of you:
my grandmother Marshall, My mother, My aunt Louise,
My Uncle Gus, and brother and sister,
long in you who still watch over this church from
a higher altar than was intended for those who sat
in the back pews: all the colored.

I sing, she celebrates outside her quiet voice,
and bring you witness from the God that brought

this song from me in full bloom,
without the geography of back pews
and choirlofts.

The Drowned River

For Rose for Michael

You told me, Rose, of this river, how the Susquehanna
submerges itself under the Chesapeake Bay
to become a drowned river.

> *He tends his pain each morning*
> *with a glance at his fragile garden,*
> *a gesture toward his tender bedroom,*
> *a look at his invisible shadow*
> *that augurs a lament in the creaking*
> *of mirrors, non-existent in his house,*
> *but haunting his memory of himself.*

> *There is a Who somewhere. Can he find it?*

The river, you say, flows powerfully under
drowning itself to create another identity
close to its own, closer to its nature,
crest to its ambivalence and the water of its ways.

The drowning is a survival.

> *He goes under at intervals, looks at the clock,*
> *knows the day is due, a premium must be paid,*
> *falters, hopes, looks for last things: a sock, a shoe,*
> *asks a vase if she's still there,*
> *if the colors are right, if there is a survival*
> *in its texture, its watching of inanimate things.*

> *The vase answers Yes.*
> *All of the above.*
> *He has named the vase after someone*

who moves about his dreams while his step
stutters on the staircase.

Where is she, this woman?
Not within his reach, swimming somewhere
under.

He wants her to rise, to surface:
his sanity depends upon it.

And she does, after she has drowned.

The river is wonderful, you say.
Its energy connects to the center of the universe.
That is why it is transformed to a greater thing.
That is why the Chesapeake smiles at hurricanes.

He wonders. He is not a swimmer. He cannot cope
with drownings. She surfaces, takes him under,
as he leaves his house, locks his door,
enters the water, stunned in her embrace.
Soon they rise.

He does his day's work at the office,
surrenders his vision into another time:
a river of the redemptive.

And knows that life regenerates itself
in a single promised moment awaiting his touch
that smiles at hurricanes.

*R*aymond R. Patterson

Harlem Suite

1

Silent, the Savoy,
where we once danced.
Dim, the Dawn Casino, where we played–
Minton's, Small's Paradise, the Renaissance,
Count Basie's, and the midnight promenade . . .

Of yesterday, what's left
but still, Red Rooster mornings,
dreams of Sugar Hill and Strivers Row,
the after-glow of Monteray and Connie's Inn,
of Baby Grand and Mandalay and Wishing Well and Wonder Bar,
and cool Alhambra nights
at Shalimar and Silver Rail and Lafayette and Odeon
–O Tree of Hope!–
and magical Apollo?

2

When my soul is weary–
      Do, Jesus!
When my heart is troubled–
      Yes, My Lord!
When my mind don't know my name–
      Have mercy, if you please!

When my soul is weary–
      Mount Calvary!
When my heart is troubled–
      Oh Salem!
When my mind don't know my name–
      St. Philip, on my knees!

I go to Church–
      Mother Zion!
      Shiloh!
      Abyssinian!

Just as I am—
        Christ of the Apostolic Faith!
And the Church cries,
        A-A-A-A-MEN!

3
Over my head—
above the siren wail,
above the incense, oils of Zion, grilled
        sausages, glistening like a bright disease,
above the open trucks where dreadlocked
        fruits and vegetables prevail,
above the mother tongues of Wolof, Harlemese, Igbo, Creole,
        Gullah, Rasta Patwa, Urdu, Spanglish, Cochin, Arabic,
        Cantonese,
above the drum of hiphop, gospel, reggae, rumba, highlife,
        blues, and gangsta rap,
above the shout of Malcolm, Marcus, Martin, Adam,
        Winnie, Nina, Sharpton, Farrakhan,
above the Congo River crowds of color
        splashing sidewalked traders, sandaled, beach
            umbrellaed,
        docked beside their battered vans,
above the corridors of kente, dayglow T-shirts, watches,
        sunshades, footwear, masks and statues, earrings, hats,
        cassettes, carpets, books, posters, polished brass and
        cowrie, herbs and nylon hair,
above the gridlocked avenues of heroes,
        late and hurrying towards African Square,
above the helicopter drone, where whispered
        radar beams interrogate the air

—a cry that will not cease:
No Justice, No Peace!
No Justice, No Peace!

4
Four centuries of
practiced devastation

brought to its current
perfection.

From that cage of fire
such beauty springs,
as takes the breath away!

Forerunner

Benjamin Banneker
looked at the stars
and saw the page in his almanac
that told how bright tomorrow was.

He saw beyond the sun's eclipse. He saw
a multitude of men in a new millennium
descend as from celestial ships
to walk an alien shore again.

He charted where the light would fall.
He marked the day by his wooden clock—
how beautiful its radiance,
How luminous and tall.

Knowing the future, he went ahead
with compass and transit to plot
the site. "Capital streets must be broad,"
he said, "—and built right!"

Baobab

For Gwendolyn Brooks

Tree-Mother
Sacred Tree Rooted in Sun and Soil
Tree of the Spirits of Children Waiting To Be Born
Tree Who Shelters Caravans
Shade Tree of the Littlest Ones, Who Never Tires of Their Songs
Tree of White, Pendulous Flowers
Tree of the Fullness of Night
Tree-Mother, we thank you
for your fruit, we thank you
for your fiber (to weave
our clothes) we thank you
for your medicine (to treat
our ills) we thank you.
Bees store in your hollows
the sweetest honey, we thank you.
Your children thank you, saying your name.
Teach us the strength of your branch and root.
Teach us the wisdom of your monumental growing.

Alvin Aubert

Nat Turner in the Clearing

                              Ashes, Lord—
But warm still from the fire that cheered us,
lighted us in this clearing where it seems
Scarcely an hour ago we feasted on
Burnt pig from our tormentor's unwilling
Bounty and charted the high purpose your
Word had launched us on. And now, my comrades
Dead, or taken; your servant, pressed by the
Bloody yelps of hounds, forsaken, save for
The stillness of the word that persists quivering
And breath-moist on his tongue: and these faint coals
Soon to be rushed to dying glow by the
Indifferent winds of miscarriage—What now,
My Lord? A priestess once, they say, could write
On leaves, unlock the time-bound spell of deeds
Undone. I let fall upon these pale remains
Your breath-moist word, preempt the winds, and give
Then now their one last glow, that some dark child
In time to come might pass this way and, in
This clearing, read and know.

James Baldwin, 1924–1987

The university is waiting to honor him
Joan Baez is talking on National Public Radio
a touching memory of her Quaker father leaving her
and her siblings a legacy of decency. Now
she's being asked a leading question one
question leading to another but she keeps
her cool. At thirteen, envying the vibrato
of the girls who got all the good singing parts
in her school she went home and quietly
massaged her adam's apple till a vibrato
appeared and now she's into song, partly
relieving me of the solemnity of elegiac
composition but not for long: the interstice

of the hummingbird as it backs off momentarily
from its flame the little fire it starts in the inverted
dome of the corn flower: words having come in the
morning James Baldwin is dead. Baez may
or may not have heard about James Baldwin
but she's singing "Amazing Grace."

Old preacher man, notorious old backslidin'
bible raiding no-show man who had me waiting
at the airport never showing, would have
loved Baez for that. But I don't mind
the waiting would've waited out the day
counting the things we'd talk about
driving as slow as the law allowed
the twenty miles or so back to the party waiting
at lunch for us downtown, destined to eat
our embarrassing fare in an aura of prescient
near-silence. For what is there to talk about now,
without Baldwin, everybody primed for Baldwin?

December 1982/Detroit

the loudspeakers saturate the world with christmas.
children prance down the aisles of department stores.
something is happening, one little girl seems to say,
something big and trembling, it takes hold of my hands
my feet my arms my legs saying somersault somersault
somersault which i am doing now, giving praise unto
the lord the ever coming prince of peace and food
and warmth and dry shoes and hand warming gloves
and bright new underclothes. praise be unto it all.
santa queries me softly, i whisper in his ear, i have
only to wait, now, and see. santa's not white this year,
he looks so strange, his dark face peering out through
those snow white whiskers and beard, his skin a lovely
dark brown, a smoothness of youth. i'm
in love with him. he reminds me of my grandfather down
in mississippi, so young looking for his age.

i feel i have only to wait, now, to wait and see.
this is 1982 and i have never been disappointed
at christmastime before. i have never worn shoes
with holes in them, either, but i do now. santa, grandfather,
is there something i don't know about this year?

*A*miri Baraka

I Am

For Addison Gayle, "The Black Aesthetic" & Abdullah Buhaina

Blues March

We are being told of the greatness
of Western Civilization
Yet Europe
is not the West

Leave England headed West
        you arrive
            in Newark,

The West is
The New World

                    not Europe

The West is
The New World

                    not Europe

The West is

            El Mundo Nuevo
            The Pan American
            Complexity
            As diversity as the routes
            & history
            of our collection

The West is The Americas
        not Europe

It is the America that the home
    boy tells, the sister we can
    see, yr wife, husband & children
Yr mama
Yr friends

Yr family
Yr closes enemies

    Are West, the quest
      The Search
      for Humanity
      still goes on

But of the Euro White Supremacists
    The Slave Masters
      Conquistadores
    Destroyers of Pharonic Egypt
      Carthage

Invaders, Destroyers of Moorish Spain
      Of African and Asian Worlds
      Creators of the Inquistition
      Christ Killers
      Murderers of thousands of Christians
         in the Coliseum
      Murderers of Spartacus
        Vandals
        Germ Mens
        DitchMen
        Boers

Destroyers of Mohodarenjo
      Tenotchitlan
      Killed Montezuma & Emiliano Zapata
      Malcolm X, Martin Luther King, even
      the Kennedies, Bobby Hutton, Fred Hampton
      Medgar Evers,

    The Aztecs
    The Incas
    The Mayans
    The Taino
    The Arawak

Conquerors
of
America

Enslaving

Humanity
in
Cannibal
Menus

Bush men living on human
flesh as public
ritual
ideology of predators
& blood covered claws

Murderers of Iraq, wd be destroyers of
the ancient Mesopotamian culture
Assassins of Sandino
Toussaint Louverture, Patrice Lamumba

Enslavers of Women
Overthrew Mother Right
Killed Socrates, Copernicus, Lincoln
John Brown & Nat Turner
Amilcar Cabral & David Sibeko

Who claim Civilization & Christianity & Philosophy as
Crucifiers who worshipped statues
till 300 AD

Who destroyed the libraries of Alexandria
the University at Timbuctoo
Who thought the wind made babies

Who say now they are the creators of Great Civilizations
        plagiarists, ignorant imitators
        claiming Geometry & the Lever

which existed 1000 years before
        they was even here
    whose great minds are thieves like
        Aristotle, Con men like
            Democritus & Anazimander
        whose Gods are the Vanilla Ice
            of Ethiopian Originals
            half dressed cave dwellers
            painted blue

Anglos (knife wielding) Saxons
    Sackers (Robbers) of Ancient Civilizations
    Vikings whose Gods were drunk and rowdy
    robbers like Conan & Wodan

    Punks like Napoleon who
    got run out of Haiti
        by Toussaint & Dessaline

        who got bum rushed out
            of Russia
        wacked out
        racist monsters
    shot the nose & mouth
        off the Sphinx
        so sick &

    anti-life & history were they
        who put Mali & Songhay &
        all Africa
        in Slave Ships

    for money, whose profits
    were numbers not visionaries

Life as a low thing
worshippers of mines not Minds
War Lovers not Peace Makers

Aint instead of Art
(Death instead of Life)
    Dog they best friend
      Ice & Snow
       Not We & Know
      Blood Suckers &
               Mother Fuckers

Love War
so much
call the history
of their civilization

The Cannon!

       in honor of Marco Polo's
        trip to China

Should we praise them
   for Dachau, for the poisoning
    of David Walker
    the Genocide of Native
      Americans
  or concentration camps
    for Japanese
     Americans

Perhaps 700 years of Irish Colonialism
   or Ghandhi's
     murder
   The Conquest of India
   The Opium Wars
   TB sheets for

Indians
or the trail of Tears

So how should we praise them?
And what should we call them?
    Who style themselves God
    Whose New World Order
    Seems old & Miltonian in that they rule
    & do not serve

But somehow the term Satan seems too narrow
  The word Devil is too limiting

But there must be some description, some appropriate
horrific
  we can coin—

Something that says liar, murderer, maniac, animal
something that indicates their importance.

In The Funk World

     If Elvis Presley/is
      King
     Who is James Brown,
      God?

John Coltrane (1926–1967)

I Love Music

"I want to be a force for real good.
In other words, I know that there are bad forces,
forces that bring suffering to others and misery to the world,
but I want to be the opposite
force. I want to be the force which is truly
for good."

Trane

Trane

Trane sd,

A force for real good, Trane. in other words. Feb '67
By july he was dead.
By july. He said in other words
he wanted to be the opposite
but by July he was dead, but he is, offering
expression a love supreme, afroblue in me singing
it all because of him
can be
screaming beauty
can be
afroblue can be
you leave me breathless
can be
       alabama
                I want to talk about you
                          my favorite things
                                  like sonny
can be
life itself, fire can be, heart explosion, soul explosion, brain
    explosion
can be. can be. can be. aggeeewheeeuheageeee. aeeegeheooouaaaa
deep deep deep
expression deep, can be
capitalism dying, can be
all, see, aggggeeeeoooo. aggrggrrgeeeoouuuu. full full full can be
empty too.
nightfall by water
round moon over slums
shit in a dropper
soft face under fingertips trembling
can be

can be
can be, trane, can be, trane, because of trane, because
world world world world

can be
sean o' casey in ireland
can be, lu hsun in china
can be,
      brecht wailing
         gorky   riffing
            langston hughes steaming
                        can be
                        trane
                      bird's main man
                    can be
        big maybelle can be
      workout workout workout
              expression
              Ogunde
              afroblue can be
all of it meaning, essence, revelation, everything together, wailing
   in unison
                  a terrible
wholeness

Sonia Sanchez

Ballad

(after the Spanish)

forgive me if i laugh
you are so sure of love
you are so young
and i too old to learn of love.

the rain exploding
in the air is love
the grass excreting her
green wax is love
and stones remembering
past steps is love,
but you. you are too young
for love
and i too old.

once. what does it matter
when or who, i knew
of love.
i fixed my body
under his and went
to sleep in love
all trace of me
was wiped away

forgive me if i smile
young heiress of a naked dream
you are so young
and i too old to learn to love.

Letter to Ezekiel Mphahlele

dear zeke,
    i've just left your house where you and rebecca served a dinner
of peace to me and my sons. the ride home is not as long as the way
i came, two centuries of hunger brought me along many detours
before i recognized your house. it is raining and as i watch the rain-

drops spin like colored beads on the windshield, i hear your voice calling out to your ancestors to prepare a place for you, for you were returning home leaving the skeleton rites of twenty years behind.

you and rebecca have been walking a long time. your feet have crossed the african continent to this western one where you moved amid leaden eyes and laughter that froze you in snow/capped memories. your journey began in 1957, when the ruling class could not understand your yawns of freedom, the motion of a million eyes to see for themselves what life was/is and could be, and you cut across the burial grounds of south africa where many of your comrades slept and you cut across those black africans smiling their long smiles from diplomatic teeth. now you are returning home. now your mother's womb cries out to you. now your history demands your heartbeat. and you turn your body toward the whirlwind of change, toward young black voices calling for a dignity speeding beyond control, on the right side of the road. but this nite full of whispering summer trees, this nite nodding with south african faces, heard you say, sonia. i must be buried in my country in my own homeland, my bones must replenish the black earth from whence they came, our bones must fertilize the ground on which we walk or we shall never walk as men and women in the 21st century.

i talked to my sons as the car chased the longlegged rain running before us. i told them that men and women are measured by their acts not by their swaggering speech or walk, or the money they have stashed between their legs. i talked to my sons about bravery outside of bruce lee grunts and jabs, outside of star wars' knights fertilizing america's green youth into continued fantasies while reality explodes in neutron boldness. i said you have just sat and eaten amid bravery. relish the taste. stir it around and around in your mouth until the quick sweetness of it becomes bitter, then swallow it slowly, letting this new astringent taste burn the throat. bravery is no easy taste to swallow. i said this man and woman we have just left this nite have decided to walk like panthers in their country, to breathe again their own breath suspended by twenty years of exile, to settle in the maternal space of their birth where there are men who "shake hands without hearts" waiting for them. they are a fixed portrait of courage.

it is 2 a.m., my children stretch themselves in dreams, kicking away the room's shadows. i stare at the nite piling in little heaps near my bed. zeke. maybe you are a madman. i a madwoman to

want to walk across the sea, to saddle time while singing a future
note. we follow the new day's breath, we answer old bruises wait-
ing to descend upon our heads, we answer screams creeping out of
holes and shells buried by memories waiting to be cleansed. you
invoking the ghosts lurking inside this child/woman. you breaking
my curtain of silence. i love the tom-tom days you are marching,
your feet rooted in the sea. save a space for me and mine zeke and
rebecca. this lost woman, who walks her own shadow for peace.

Under a Soprano Sky

1
once i lived on pillars in a green house
boarded by lilacs that rocked voices into weeds.
i bled an owl's blood
shredding the grass until i
rocked in a choir of worms.
obscene with hands, i wooed the world
with thumbs
                while yo-yos hummed.
was it an unborn lacquer i peeled?
the woods, tall as waves, sang in mixed
tongues that loosened the scalp
and my bones wrapped in white dust
returned to echo in my thighs.

i heard a pulse wandering somewhere
on vague embankments.
O are my hands breathing? I cannot smell the nerves.
i saw the sun
ripening green stones for fields.
O have my eyes run down? i cannot taste my birth.

2
now as i move, mouth quivering with silks
my skin runs soft with eyes.
descending into my legs, i follow obscure birds
purchasing orthopedic wings.
the air is late this summer.

i peel the spine and flood
the earth with adolescence.
O who will pump these breasts? I cannot waltz my tongue.

under a soprano sky, a woman sings,
lovely as chandeliers.

For Sweet Honey in the Rock

I'm gonna stay on the battlefield
I'm gonna stay on the battlefield
I'm gonna stay on the battlefield til I die.

I'm gonna stay on the battlefield
I'm gonna stay on the battlefield
I'm gonna stay on the battlefield til I die.

i had come into the city carrying life in my eyes
amid rumors of death,
calling out to everyone who would listen
it is time to move us all into another century
time for freedom and racial and sexual justice
time for women and children and men time for hands unbound
i had come into the city wearing peaceful breasts
and the spaces between us smiled
i had come into the city carrying life in my eyes.
i had come into the city carrying life in my eyes.

And they followed us in their cars with their computers
and their tongues crawled with caterpillars
and they bumped us off the road turned over our cars,
and they bombed our buildings killed our babies,
and they shot our doctors maintaining our bodies,
and their courts changed into confessionals
but we kept on organizing we kept on teaching believing
loving doing what was holy moving to a higher ground
even though our hands were full of slaughtered teeth
but we held out our eyes delirious with grace.
but we held out our eyes delirious with grace.

I'm gonna treat everybody right
I'm gonna treat everybody right
I'm gonna treat everybody right til I die.

I'm gonna treat everybody right
I'm gonna treat everybody right
I'm gonna treat everybody right til I die.

come. i say come, you sitting still in domestic bacteria
come. i say come, you standing still in double-breasted mornings
come. i say come, and return to the fight.
this fight for the earth
this fight for our children
this fight for our life
we need your hurricane voices
we need your sacred hands

i say, come, sister, brother to the battlefield
come into the rain forests
come into the hood
come into the barrio
come into the schools
come into the abortion clinics
come into the prisons
come and caress our spines

i say come, wrap your feet around justice
i say come, wrap your tongues around truth
i say come, wrap your hands with deeds and prayer
you brown ones
you yellow ones
you black ones
you gay ones
you white ones
you lesbian ones

Comecomecomecomecome to this battlefield
called life, called life, called life . . . .

I'm gonna stay on the battlefield
I'm gonna stay on the battlefield
I'm gonna stay on the battlefield til I die.

I'm gonna stay on the battlefield
I'm gonna stay on the battlefield
I'm gonna stay on the battlefield til I die.

Philadelphia: Spring, 1985

1
/a phila. fireman reflects after
seeing a decapitated body in the MOVE ruins/

to see those eyes
orange like butterflies
over the walls.

i must move away
from this little-ease
where the pulse
shrinks into itself
and carve myself in white.

O to press the seasons
and taste the quiet juice
of their veins.

2/*memory*/
a
Thus in the varicose town
where eyes splintered the night with glass
the children touched at random
sat in places where legions rode.

And O we watched the young birds
stretch the sky
until it streamed white ashes
and O we saw mountains lean on seas
to drink the blood of whales
then wander dumb with their wet bowels.

b
Everywhere young
faces breathing in crusts.

breakfast of dreams.
The city, lit by a single fire,
followed the air into disorder.
And the sabbath stones singed our eyes
with each morning's coin.

c

Praise of a cureless death they heard
without confessor;
Praise of cathedrals
pressing their genesis from priests;
Praise of wild gulls who came and drank
their summer's milk,
then led them toward the parish snow.

How still the spiderless city.
The earth is immemorial in death.

For Sister Gwen Brooks

you tell the stars
don't be jealous of her light
you tell the ocean,
you call out to Olukun,
to bring her always to
safe harbor,
for she is a holy one
this woman twirling
her emerald lariat
you tell the night
to move gently
into morning so she's
not startled,
you tell the morning
to ease her into a water
fall of dreams
for she is a holy one
restringing her words
from city to city

so that we live and
breathe and smile and
breathe and love and
breathe her . . .
this Gwensister called life.

Lucille Clifton

dialysis

after the cancer, the kidneys
refused to continue.
they closed their thousand eyes.

blood fountains from the blind man's
arm and decorates the tile today.
somebody mops it up.

the woman who is over ninety
cries for her mother. if our dead
were here they would save us.

we are not supposed to hate
the dialysis unit. we are not
supposed to hate the universe.

this is not supposed to happen to me.
after the cancer the body refused
to lose any more. even the poisons
were claimed and kept

until they threatened to destroy
the heart they loved. in my dream
a house is burning.

something crawls out of the fire
cleansed and purified.
in my dream i call it light.

after the cancer i was so grateful
to be alive. i am alive and furious.
Blessed be even this?

donor

to lex

when they tell me that my body
might reject

i think of thirty years ago
and the hangers i shoved inside
hard trying to not have you.

i think of the pills, the everything
i gathered against your
inconvenient bulge; and you
my stubborn baby child,
hunched there in the dark
refusing my refusal.

suppose my body does say no
to yours. again, again i feel you
buckled in despite me, lex,
fastened to life like the frown
on an angel's brow.

1994

i was leaving my fifty-eighth year
when a thumb of ice
stamped itself near my heart

you have your own story
you know about the fear the tears
the scar of disbelief

you know the saddest lies
are the ones we tell ourselves
you know how dangerous it is

to be born with breasts
you know how dangerous it is
to wear dark skin

i was leaving my fifty-eighth year
when i woke into the winter
of a cold and mortal body

thin icicles hanging off
the one mad nipple weeping

have we not been good children
did we not inherit the earth

but you must know all about this
from your own shivering life

Jayne Cortez

There It Is

My friend
they don't care
if you're an individualist
a leftist   a rightist
a shithead or a snake

They will try to exploit you
absorb you   confine you
disconnect you   isolate you
or kill you

And you will disappear into your own rage
into your own insanity
into your own poverty
into a word a phrase a slogan a cartoon
and then ashes

The ruling class will tell you that
there is no ruling class
as they organize their liberal supporters into
white supremist lynch mobs
organize their children into
ku klux klan gangs
organize their police into
killer cops
organize their propaganda into
a device to ossify us with angel dust
pre-occupy us with western symbols in
african hair styles
innoculate us with hate
institutionalize us with ignorance
hypnotize us with a monotonous sound designed
to make us evade reality and stomp our lives away
And we are programmed to self destruct
to fragment
to get buried under covert intelligence operations of
unintelligent committees impulsed toward death
And there it is

The enemies polishing their penises between
oil wells at the pentagon
the bulldozers leaping into demolition dances
the old folks dying of starvation
the informers wearing out shoes looking for crumbs
the lifeblood of the earth almost dead in
the greedy mouth of imperialism
And my friend
they don't care
if you're an individualist
a leftist   a rightist
a shithead or a snake

They will spray you with
a virus of legionnaire's disease
fill your nostrils with
the swine flu of their arrogance
stuff your body into a tampon of
toxic shock syndrome
try to pump all the resources of the world
into their own veins
and fly off into the wild blue yonder to
pollute another planet

And if we don't fight
if we don't resist
if we don't organize and unify and
get the power to control our own lives
Then we will wear
the exaggerated look of captivity
the stylized look of submission
the bizzare look of suicide
the dehumanized look of fear
and the decomposed look of repression
forever and ever and ever

The Guitars I Used to Know

Guitars
with excavated rhythms

with maps & bridges
& the sweetness of sugar from
        Pernambuco
      from Nacogdoches
   from Itta Bena
from Chitunguiza
Guitars
with names like
  Edolia Adelia
   Freddie Mae Johnny Boy
Matakenya Machado
  Zodwa & Letty Bea
Guitars
Guitars full of
inlaid shark fins
apocalyptic blood-stained finger boards
intoxicated paradoxinated coils
indigenous fusionous realms
collisional digital switches
reverse reverb shrills on flat-bed trucks
   Guitars
The guitars trembling into
ultrasonic tempos into
insurrectional gestures into
scrunching wild dog yowls
Yowling
with the mother-of-pearl habit
of living in isolation
with the plastic tradition
of being too sociable
with the inflammatory projections
hyperventilating into
trances stances romances
Guitars
The guitars I used to know
Guitars
arriving from Chicago
from Takaradi
from Casamance
from Texas
from Toledo

& I can hear
the guitars calling themselves Lightnin'
I can hear the guitars calling themselves T Bone
I can hear the guitars calling themselves Minnie
& I can hear the black laquered guitars
& the red guitars & the big brown rusty guitars
& cadillac green guitars & majestic purple guitars
& metallic blue   Guitars
accoustically dipping down whispering
'Don't make me wait too long now'   Guitars
electronically screaming
'I heard you beating your lover last night'   Guitars
zigzagging through the crowd & shouting
'I'm not losing my mind over you baby'   Guitars
marching around & yelling
'I'm gonna cut your power line'   Guitars
turning flips & whining
like ritual killers   Guitars
vamping on bandstands
& laughing like howler monkeys   Guitars
clearing paths
& humming like violins from Swaziland   Guitars
hollering half tone half step higher than
ordinary catastrophes   Guitars
circling with strings on teeth & crying ouch
Guitars
gigless   strapless
hanging upside-down like
disembodied robots
between dilapidated flamenco boots
exhausted pubic bones
& torn alligator shoe tongues
Guitars
hanging upside-down while
people imitate specialty of
the next machine   Guitars hanging
upside-down before resurrecting & exploding
straight out into the air
of numb thumbs
of snap slaps
of steel squeals

of moan zones
of pecked necks
of drill trills
of joke smoke
of set frets
of ride slides
of squeeze freeze
of plunk funk
of ping ting
of jam slam slam slam slam slam
        slam slam slam
Guitars
The guitars I used to know

The Heavy Headed Dance

For Mel & Ted

I am dancing &
on my head
is the spotted skunk
whose scent did not protect it
from Mr. & Mrs. Archibald of Texas

On my head
is the stuffed bobcat
whose facial expression was set
by the taxidermy department

On my head
is a bull caught
in the act of masturbation
& on top of that
rides the moose
stunned-gunned while wading in a lake
& on top of that
are the monkeys
entrapped while urinating
& on top of that
lay the hyena

jackal & vulture
shot while eating from zebra carcasses
& on top of that
sits the ram with
largest horn on record
donated by Henry Beck
& with all the stuffed animals piled on my head
I am dancing past
lyricist with the baboon heart

I am dancing like a dog
in front of financial consultant
implanted with pig genes

I am dancing & fluttering like a butterfly
across from novelist posing
in a beaver skin coat

I am dancing near the astronomer
who circles the floor with her
uplifting face frozen like a tiger

I am dancing against window
of artificial coyotes
& howling with contemporary African band
in the grizzly bear room

I am dancing my pangolin hairdo dance
past the river of ants in panties
of gyrating vocal groups

I am dancing so many different dances
with so many bloated animals
dead on my head
that my head is
a dancing museum of unnatural history
& I am dancing where I cannot see
myself dancing to know
why I am dancing
but I am dancing
I am dancing

Eugene B. Redmond

New York Seizures

For Raymond Patterson

#1

I sit in a glass submarine
Watching contortion consume beauty:
     as flesh inches toward dust and oblivion,
     . . . a-what-a-ya-wanna, eh!? a-what-a-ya-wanna!
     As flesh inches toward the next corner of tumult–
To where wrinkled octogenarians,
     Spontaneous in their gloom,
Stagger-stab the grimacing city blocks
With lock-legged steps;
And broken winds exhale columns of creaking
Epilogues from eyes without age . . .

     No dozer, no-doze city never-wink wailer,
     Babbling through your Benzedrine and beer!

#2

Now disguised as a street lamp,
I am whiplashed/whiplashed into serpentine ecstasy
By lush scenarios
By concrete choruses
     And asphalt furies:
By the snaking quarrel of bi-lingual taxi-cabs–

     Where the night turns yellow!
     Where New York gets mel-looow!

–And perspiring tenements:

     Toombs for pre-people returning home
     From mystical voyages to be somebody;

By the hover-clusters of chuckling midgets
Who hurl diabolical ringshouts under thunder-tears
of Gleeful gods: Apollo, Shango, John Henry & Bobo–
And rocket naughty clichés at bronze brickhouses,
Headhunters

Plush stallions,
Stark-denyers of identities,
Penis-flingers
Cunt-lubricators,
Sweetboys
& Blood-borrowers:

> *eenie meenie mynie mo las night/night befo*
> *spin yo bottom shoot yo shot keep her'n creep her*
> *let me blues ya fo I lose ya let me try ya*
> *'fo I buy ya I got the jones 'nnn if you got*
> *the bones dick haarrddd as Chinese Arithmetic*
> *ya know I ain't tawkin bout yo momma wit hu good*
> *o soul . . . uh uhhh! uh uhhhh! uh uhhhhhhh!*

#3
The neighbor nextdoor is hallucinating:
Woman says she saw a BlackJesus riding in a WhiteHog
Wearing a Green jumpsuit and holding two BrownFoxes;
A platinum barrel of death stares into the stomach
Of a short-order cook demanding the cashregister & life—*to go!*
A gentleman who wears low profiles tells his woman
That she makes love like his best buddy;
A Puerto Rican speaks Voodoo with an African accent;
A European speaks African with a Spanish accent;
A West Indian yawns in Yiddish and curses in Arabic;
An African speaks English in silence;
A slave revolt occurs under the cover of a blackout;
Color-crossed lovers hold hands in cross-eyed Central Park;
Subway trains are flying nonStop to South Africa;
Harlem has received the Nobel Prize for Peace;
Mountain climbers are trying to scale the City Debt;
The Indians are hijacking the Empire State Building;
This winter's snow turns out to co-caine.

#4
Lucid lumbrous eye
        New York;
Luminous fragments,
        Like New Year's Eve tin-foils,
        Collect into an epidemic of flesh-ignited candles

That refuse to go out—
Even when the temperamental gods of Con-Edison are comatose;

Whir-City,heat forest
Of memorable fevers,
      Asphalt icon:

Jezzibel mesmerizer,
Sleep-exempt entrancer:
I rap-prance my congratulations on the achievement of your
excellent
      madness,
On the triumph of your pretty contradictions;
I tap-dance my salutes through your basement of shuttles and
barbiturates;
I clop-clop along your rib-cage of cobblestones;
I pee-pee in the wee-wee hours of your doorways;
I mee-lee in your disco-drudgery;
I be-me in your awesome amber:

      No dozer, no-doze city & never-wink wailer,
      Babbling through your Benzedrine and beer!

11-haiku-poem for a magnificent million

In memoriam: for village marchers Taylor Jones III,
Homer Randolph & Stanford Tucker

east saint africa
swoons to Farrakhan's croon of
home-toned conch/us/ness

sidekicks & convoys
hitch dreams to jazz-blue histrees,
freeways, cb's, clouds

chocolate city's
manrise on a sunless mall
g/hosting MLK

joy drums joy & floods
a million-eyed ensemble
atoning/intoning/toned

mumia, malcolm
spar for friendly battle-space
on placards, tee-shirts

puberty brigades
trumpet the millennium
at miles davis school

heroes hug heroes;
bards, bloods & mentors remix
stew of umoja

drums: batteries that
flesh october words ntu
kwanzaa-yule blues hues

now, turn the year's curve:
hip-slip ntu black histree's
million year mystery

june/bug's soundz thread
east saint arkansas's 3rd eye:
summer's up-south trek

open mike poets
duel death in villagers' ears
w/rapped in drum roll's scroll

*M*ichael S. Harper

Dear John, Dear Coltrane

                    a love supreme, a love supreme
                    a love supreme, a love supreme

Sex fingers toes
in the marketplace
near your father's church
in Hamlet, North Carolina—
witness to this love
in this calm fallow
of these minds,
there is no substitute for pain:
genitals gone or going,
seed burned out,
you tuck the roots in the earth,
turn back, and move
by river through the swamps,
singing: *a love supreme, a love supreme;*
what does it all mean?
Loss, so great each black
woman expects your failure
in mute change, the seed gone.
You plod up into the electric city—
your song now crystal and
the blues. You pick up the horn
with some will and blow
into the freezing night:
a love supreme, a love supreme—

Dawn comes and you cook
up the thick sin 'tween
impotence and death, fuel
the tenor sax cannibal
heart, genitals and sweat
that makes you clean—
a love supreme, a love supreme—

Why you so black?
cause I am
why you so funky?

cause I am
why you so black?
cause I am
why you so sweet?
cause I am
why you so black?
cause I am
a love supreme, a love supreme:

So sick
you couldn't play *Naima,*
so flat we ached
for song you'd concealed
with your own blood,
your diseased liver gave
out its purity,
the inflated heart
pumps out, the tenor kiss,
tenor love:
a love supreme, a love supreme—
a love supreme, a love supreme—

Last Affair: Bessie's Blues Song

Disarticulated
arm torn out,
large veins cross
her shoulder intact,
her tourniquet
her blood in all-white big bands:

Can't you see
what love and heartache's done to me
I'm not the same as I used to be
this is my last affair

Mail truck or parked car
in the fast lane,
afloat at forty-three

on a Mississippi road,
Two-hundred-pound muscle on her ham bone,
'nother nigger dead 'fore noon:

Can't you see
what love and heartache's done to me
I'm not the same as I used to be
this is my last affair

Fifty-dollar record
cut the vein in her neck,
fool about her money
toll her black train wreck,
white press missed her fun'ral
in the same stacked deck:

Can't you see
what love and heartache's done to me
I'm not the same as I used to be
this is my last affair

Loved a little blackbird
heard she could sing,
Martha in her vineyard,
pestle in her spring,
Bessie had a bad mouth
made my chimes ring:

Can't you see
what love and heartache's done to me
I'm not the same as I used to be
this is my last affair

High Modes: Vision as Ritual: Confirmation

Black Man Go Back To The Old Country
Black Man Go Back To The Old Country
Black Man Go Back To The Old Country
Black Man Go Back To The Old Country

And you went back home for the images,
the brushwork packing the mud
into the human form; and the ritual:
Black Man Go Back To The Old Country.

We danced, the chocolate trees and samba
leaves wetting the paintbrush, and babies
came in whispering of one, oneness,
otherness, forming each man in his music,
one to one: and we touched, *contact-high,*
high modes, *contact-high,* and the images,
contact-high, man to man, came back.
Black Man Go Back To The Old Country.

The grooves turned in a human face,
Lady Day, blue and green, modally,
and we touched, *contact-high,* high modes:
Black Man Go Back To The Old Country.

Bird was a mode from the old country;
Bud Powell bowed in modality, blow Bud;
Louis Armstrong touched the old country,
and brought it back, around corners;
Miles is a mode; Coltrane is, power,
Black Man Go Back To The Old Country
Black Man Go Back To The Old Country
Black Man Go Back To The Old Country.

And we go back to the well: Africa,
the first mode, and man, modally,
touched the land of the continent,
modality: we are one; a man is another
man's face, modality, in continuum,
from man, to man, *contact-high,* to man,
contact-high, to man, high modes, oneness,
contact-high, man to man, *contact-high:*

Black Man Go Back To The Old Country
Black Man Go Back To The Old Country
Black Man Go Back To The Old Country
Black Man Go Back To The Old Country.

Askia M. Touré

Summer Worlds: A Mythic Landscape

For Jerry Fluellen, Seer

I

Where are the Summer Worlds
      we shared when dawn dazzled
      our infant-eyes?
      Babyhearts beat firmly
      then on the bedrock of
      ecstasy.
Summer Worlds shimmering at the edge
of consciousness. Time faded, trapped within
cells of lost magics. Babyeyes embracing Mystery
simply as a cat stretches simple curves under
morning skies.   Summer Worlds
      we hear you call
      us, softly under vivid yesterskies
      diamond-sparkle stars sing in
      harmony/nightvoices lush in moist
      dusk softly after rain,
Will we find you again? Pale aryans freed
Time, crushed lost magics. Their day screams along
our unprotected nerve ends. Their harsh music
      screams dull hatreds:
      heaven stormed and raped under
      phallic rocketships;
      winterhearts wallowing in snowscapes
      computer-minds programmed to measure
      everything.   Love
      dismembered. Sweaty palms grasp
      the woman, Mystery, crush her
      under bellowing lust.
      Apemen prevail, pursue
      the autumn wind, prevent
      innocence from birthing wonder.

II

Summer Worlds, where are you?
Do you call when shadows fall
across lost patterns of the stars?

We sigh and magic whispers
        down muted melodies,
        mysteries merge with
        shimmering dreams.

Where and when will you
come to us again? Your love
reflected as golden moons
   in quiet lakes.
        Your love
        singing soft songs
        on heights
        above lost cities.
        Your eyes brilliant black,
        khol-rimmed as Egypt,
        as the Woman, whole again,
living in this solo. Summer Worlds,
        I smile in recognition, poets
        resurrect your song in our music
        wild again within our lives.

        Soon Mystery will
        reign anew, as we rise
        to make a world emerge
        from shimmering dreams.
        Summer Worlds, we love you
        Summer Worlds, return
        to us   Summer Worlds
             Summer Worlds . . .

NOTES: "Summer Worlds" is a symbolic, mythical poem describing the Fall of the ancient world, which is known as the Bronze Age, dominated by the Nile Valley civilization, and led by ancient Kemet (Egypt) and Kuxh (Ethiopia). The title "Summer Worlds" refers to the tropical regions of the earth (Africa and southern Asia, which had no Ice Age to retard human progress) that produced humanity's archetypal civilizations. These remarkable cultures were destroyed by Aryan invasions, first by Assyrians, then by Persians, and later by Macedonian Greeks, under Alexander the Great.

This "timeless" age of wonders was created by the spiritual architects, or master builders, of the African mystery schools, under the aspects of Isis, the black Madonna, symbolized by the woman, who was considered sacred and named Throne of Kemet and Guardian of all Knowledge, including science and the arts.

Ab*original* Elegy: The Once and Future Queen

Glisten in your pristine splendor,
Mosetta, my dear.
Your magnificent indigo/ebony
is an ab*original* epic written
in melanin; Isis of Beginnings:
Archetypal Image preceding
"Eve" and the Semite World!
You are seed of the legendary Great Mother,
Whose munificence nurtured the "Naked Ape."
Ancient Evenings smile with the glow
of your brilliant teeth embraced by
the regal chalice of full lips,
pleasuring my moods, assuaging
volcanic expressions; causing a cool,
Nile inundation
        to soothe my Maroon passion,
                as I
            contemplate
        a Palmares future . . .

You are Twin-souled/
                Double-faced:
mythic Enchantress, modern Enhancer
of Africentric Survival Wisdom;
Primordial Womb-land personified:
the Bimsha and the Goddess:
Nefertari and Ciseley Tyson,
Hatshepsut and Bessie Smith,
Amenirdis and Gladys Knight:
the Ancient World remembered;
the Modern World enkindled
by your
        Protracted Consistency, your
Spiritual Impregnability, your
spell-binding, unsung Beauty
embodied in a peacock
Cornucopia of color!
Stun us with your

scarlet, mauve, vermilion,
tangerine, aqua, emerald.
Mesmerize us with your
Cake Walk, Black Bottom,
Shimmy, Lindy Hop, Boo-
ga-loo, Shing-aling,
ostrich plumes, bangles and beads;
your midnight-sexy panther strut,
arching buttocks shimmying
like velvet gelatin!

And yet, a certain "temperate"
temperament would eradicate
your tropical presence,
like String Quartets–
or Muzak–liquidating
the Blues, like
Calvinist hymns
erasing Spirituals,
like New Orleans bishops
slandering Marie Laveaux,
like Lawrence Welk
dethroning
the Duke of Ellington . . .

You are absent as Image
in the "Nordicized" Media,
forever boring us with
renovated myths of *Goldilocks*–
as beach girl and fantasy lover,
"peach-skinned" model and starlet,
Adnauseum.   Yet,
                  every living day,
we observe you moving swiftly,
with rhythmic, hypnotic grace,
through busy urbanscapes,
as though pursuing
a lost grandeur.
All of that dynamic, charismatic
glory–real, living,
      warm–shocking us

deeply
into Memory/
Archetypal
ecstasy . . .

Yes, unsung, "invisible,"
the ab*original* queen endures;
while we contemplate your classic
beauty, like Tarharqa . . .
gazing with streaming eyes
from far Napata,
>while Aryans rape
>his darling Khemi:
>Her indigo glory
>lost to him/
>>Forever!

NOTES: Palmares, or Os Palmares, was the African republic established by slave-rebels in seventeenth-century Brazil. It lasted for almost a century, despite attempts by several Portuguese armies to destroy it.

Bimsha. In Afri-Caribbean parlance, a beautiful, jet-black woman.

Tarharqa. The last Nubian pharoah of the twenty-fifth Dynasty, who tried to save Kemet (Egypt) from the barbaric Assyrians, who plundered and destroyed the ancient empire (metaphorically feminized as Khemi in the poem).

Napata. The ancient capital of the Nubians, located south of Kemet. Tarharqa was forced to retreat to Napata with his royal house, while helplessly watching ancient Kemet raped, plundered, degraded, and destroyed.

O Lord of Light! A Mystic Sage Returns to Realms of Eternity!

For Master Sun Ra/Sonny Blount
May 22, 1914–May 30, 1993

I

He is sun-bright myth and Cosmic Light,
the audaciousness of comets sweeping through the inky abyss
of night,
the Solar Lord as pharoah of magic, mega-sounds, harmonious
with spectacular delights and unbridaled flights aboard

the Melanin rocketship bound for the funk planets.
Ja man of Jupiterian wisdom, crowned prince of immortal night:
Lord Sun-Ra renamed,
renowned, resplendent in sparkling, sequined satins;
solar disc ablaze like a living Uraeus, working his aural magic
among the tropic myths of reborn Kamites. In the kingdoms
of his liberated soul, in realms of resurgent Negritude, we
celebrate his audacity, his expanded vision of
Possibility; moving beyond plastic parameters
of Anglo blandness, into multidimensional
space-time continuums,
restoring the broad-ranged, epic Consciousness of Cosmic Music,
embodied in a galaxy of master compositions, Alchemical
solos featuring Coltrane and Pharoah,
Don and Albert Ayler, Ornette Coleman, Sunny Murray, Milford
Graves,
Marion Brown and myriad masters embracing
sacred pillars of the Sky Lords, Immortal Mansions of Ra.

II
He has moved beyond us, riding Shango's lightning into stellar
parameters; a Moon Lord, changing his coat
arrayed in cosmic colors; hanging with Tehuti, embracing azure
robes
of Isis, soloing with Bird Diz Miles among expanses of
inter-galactic
space ways, riding bursts of super-novas
brighter than a million mushroom bombs. A living Ancestor now
with Larry Neal, Henry Dumas
legendary visionaries embodying all of our
sterling strengths, imaginative flights, volcanic passion, spanning
generations of Captivity and Resistance, deep pain
wild joy—the Cosmic Lord resplendent among us;
solar obelisk of myth, long-breath solo of God-voice surging in
symphonies of light, phoenix flight of bright Bennu, delighting
myriad choruses of angels, Orishas, who
dance upon sun beams of his extended solos: O Lord of Light,
O Sun Prince transporting our tropic memories to emerald
mountains rising above primordial jungle dawns;
O Sky Lord roaring a Horus mantra in a dark abyss of Caucasian-
Neanderthal hell;

O Father, Osirian mage waving your pharoanic baton above
choruses of
saxophones, possees of trumpets, bevies of thundering Afrikan
drums
shaking the earth like Zulu legions.

III

We mourn you when Whirlwinds roar and embrace our Marcus
Garvey
rhapsodies above Middle Passage moans;
We mourn you when Midnight glides into our Consciousness
wearing
a white gardenia above her
Billie Holiday face; when Sassy Vaughn launches her indigo-
velvet
voice upon that mantras of our ecstasies.
We sing you, Father Ra-Osiris, asking that our memories continue
in your voyages to farthest reaches of the Universe, that they
form a ring around your Solar Disc as
monumental love vibrations; for you are our heart, our elder sage
and parent, our cosmological thrust into parameters of Infinity,
an epiphany of Cosmic compassion
mounting summits of Divinity, an archetypal surge of Harmony
within temples of Maatic Eternity;
in Pyramids and mythic shadows, in sunbursts of meteor showers,
in Whirlwinds riding glowing episodes of ritual Nirvana; O Sage,
we wish you long life in transcendental vistas
amid pristine solos raising the Dead;
We ask that Ra, mounting
His Barque of Millions of Years, welcome His son
into infinite realms of joy, Mansions
of the Cosmic Light!

NOTES: Uraeus. A representation of the sacred asp on the headdress of Kemetic
(Egyptian) rulers symbolizing sovereignty.

Kamites. From Kamit or Kemet (the Black Land). The Kamites were the black
people of the Black Land.

Ra. Ancient Kemetic (Egyptian) for Almighty God, whose sacred symbol was
the sun, as the light of the universe.

Shango. West African, Yoruba orisha symbolizing kingship, whose sacred pres-
ence was embodied in thunder and lightning bolts.

Tehuti (Thoth, Greek). The Kemetic neter who symbolized knowledge, ancient wisdom, mystery, measurement of the heavens, and phases of the moon.

Isis (Greek for Auset). The Nile Valley civilization's Great Mother, Queen of Heaven, Throne of Kemet, the queen and coruler with King Asar (Osiris, Greek). Humanity's archetypal black Madonna.

Larry Neal, Henry "Ankh" Dumas. Two outstanding African American visionary epic poets, leaders in the 1960s Black Arts cultural era.

Obelisk. (Greek). For a monolithic, four-sided Egyptian pillar that tapers into a pyramid, symbolic of pharoanic authority.

Bennu (Kemetic). The original divine bird that served as archetype for the later Greek bird, the phoenix.

Orishas. Divine Beings of the West African Yorubas, paralleling the Kemetic neters and the Christian/Hebrew/ Muslim angels.

*S*terling D. Plumpp

Be-Bop

Be-Bop is precise clumsiness.
   Awkward lyricism
   under a feather's control.
A world in a crack.
Seen by ears.
   Von Freeman's
tenor Apocalypses/beginning
skies fussy about air and protective
   of trombones on Jacob's Ladder
   strung from basses
in a corner of handclaps.
Drums praying over evil
   done by trumpets
   and dances in fingertips.
Be-Bop is elusive hammerlocks
a piano accords crescendos
   in blue moanings.
Lingers in beats marching
   across faces of sense.
Harmonic nightmares obeying
   pianissimos of tones
erupting from barks of Powell.
Be-Bop is unexpected
   style punching music
with garlic in tempo.

     Billie's pain
     and a cup of insinuations
     drunk by laughter
     before tears arise.

History, Hollers, and Horn

All
the voices in the universe
I contact I

speak

when
I solo on voyages in
to selves in
side my
self I need
to explore

My
axe is not the Enola Gay
so it does
not huff or
puff away places

It
seizes with eyes piercing
skin of clouds
or moral codes It does
not invite light of a thousand light
years at its front door
way to where black
rain falls like Dinah's
blues on this bit of earth
quakes

I
belong to a land of
a thousand dances

and
my axe is not the Enola Gay
chaps or gals at the bar
be cued shadow of a hundred
thousand or more

at Hiroshima or
Nagasaki where language
failed to enchant veins
with songs

All
ways I travel knowing
the language I seek is with
in a universe in
side me where
on the day I was born
I
knew I would never know
the entire history of my horn

Spirituals and toasts
and field
hollers and blues
and sermons and
swing and Dixie
land and be
bop are stops on the road
I travel

where I know
I will never know
the entire geography of
my horn

But I
will come out
each night and I will solo

and travel where
ever my horn leads me
on let me stand

Ornate with Smoke

Remaking:
a distinguished breakage.

The
fountain of language

discoursing with every
day feet. In postures of
wings. Stem of a tongue
rising from debris of a
Trane ornate with smoke.

Short
bursts of air signify. A century of
silence recoiled
in tenor moments you
revive. Velvet totems of faces
you wear. Ricocheted touches.
Jamming with masks of iron
and thunder tap
dancing with rattling
feats of rhythms.

You
have been here
before.

And I

know you from hemorrhages of light
years. I hear Miles
down hives of the Be
bopping itch to create.

Avalanches I prepare.
Atoms I raise.
Clouds I mime.
Montages of demons I translate.

I pursue languages of my foot
step children of swing in Dixie
land or at Minton's.

Dissonance
is a ventriloquist calling
my speech from dry bones
through silent drums. Down to McCall's
voice.

Is the do
rag common
denominator of riffing paths
through nights of bone mountains.

I chew terrible bubble gum
bo arrows of speech.
I order from Mingus's catalogs
of tonight at noon
or Ornette's tomorrow.
Tonight is
the night I be
head youth.

Cryptic dialogues of alien
greetings in chords are slaps on my back
water blues. I drink muddy
logic sleep in cold
train's box
cars of innovative ceilings. I adjust.

I do
not need to sign an agreement of
unity with a foreign
language. In order to speak my mother
tongue.

I
come from death and after
thoughts. Of another life on chromatic planes of
How I Got Over and No Hiding Place and Strange
Fruits. I pick from vine
yards of Birds and Counts and Dukes and Poppa
Got Brand New Bags of maps.
I file in my imagination.

I
find staples of my diet in hors d'oeuvres.
On kaleidoscopic menus of chance
and my axe leases an apartment
from tenements of pain

and begin teaching sultry
liaisons with a geography.
Circumscribed by holy
rollers and the mighty rock
church inventions of shouts.
In the face of bleeding ulcers of
forecasts of rain on my days.

A generation robbed.
Of its cacophony
is illiterate.

I got black cat
a combs in dread
locks of the Rubic
on off nights I back
stroke to back
beats of Handy melodies
I feel and shout:

Yo
rub a belly of dialects
I name with windows I
open with riffs of a good
morning glory
I offer

Nommo auction clocks
for me
Nommo auction clocks
for me
Nommo auction clocks
for me

I watch my shadow perform
at rodeo stations of the cross
my dreams rise from membranes of
thieves to sing

Nommo auction clocks
for me

I am an old seventy-eight
My forty-fives are empty
The thirty-third and
one third degree of
my father's masonry
spins meandering in unemployment
lines

Nommo
Nommo
Nommo

I am responsible for language
I live
in The A Cappella Dew
Drop Inn
where I hear years of silences
shift into drive

As Malachi, the Calysonian of Rhythms,
pastes his colors betwixt
between pulses of blood
on the corner of jive and Mister Down
Child

The Judge
gives me ninety-nine
years on Parchment Farm
and I harvest signatures of dust
jackets I wear

I wake
in little E
we we hours of screaming

Give me
a glass of Rum
boogie at Basin
Street car salvage
missions

I am locked out
done lost McKie's

Throw me
out my juke boxer
shorts so I can improvise
this ring

By
the dawn's early Light
Henry Huffing and puffing
to heal
some brother inflicted
by white
rejection but exhibiting
symptoms of cancer

I wear
a Crown
Propeller on my little finger
for good lucky
strikes down lanes of white
approval but I fail

I find VeeJay data
bases in the Regal voices do
woping and motowning high
ways I travel
till the Sun
Ra boats of oarsmen
orchestrate paradigms of high
hat blues talking trash
in broken accents of salutations
in other galaxies

where I staff light
years for the good
times

I am just Da
homey a long ways

from my home
land
lords

I build settlement
hospices for old days

Yo
rub a dialect
I bring from sounds I heave
Yo
rub a language I sling
between rocks I use
as pillows

I am just Da
homey a long ways
from home
I am just Da
homey a long ways
from home

Strike
a match to hear my sound
Strike
a match to hear my sound

I am broke and alone
I am always prism bound.

from Mary

6
I wonder
where will my children
get milk
cause my cow is skinny
and ain't got
no calf

I wonder
where will my children
get milk
cause my cow is skinny
and ain't got
no calf

They
can collect a bucket full
of tears and drink
Lawd till they laugh

So as I watch
you retreat from
laughter that signifies
joy and shouts
and devilment
you grow in
side affirmations
of long rainy nights

evil knife
toting cotton
bolls and open fields
of longings
you follow

I long for stories
I know as you

Railroad crossing
Railroad crossing

Place I always at
when it rains

Railroad crossing
Railroad crossing

Place I always at
when it rains

My dreams
can't jump on
but off jump a thousand
hoboing pains

7

Daybreak wakes
my pains in the morning
Sunset reads
to my hurts
at night

Daybreak wakes
my pains in the morning
Sunset reads
to my hurts
at night

Worry
Worry

all the time
no matter
if it's in the dark
or in the light

I got
this liberated anger
under house
arrest in my songs

And I know
it is no "Magnificat"

a black girl sings a
cross Mississippi hills
mud and red
clay choruses
throbbing with blisters

hoes dish
water and low
down men bring

And I can
not say a rosary
for you since
the only beads
you know

are knots
side your head
and columned
on your spirit

My dreams
just little birds
jumping from trees
to die

My dreams
just little birds
jumping from trees
to die

Got
no pretty colored
feathers on their wings
to make them fit
to fly

Toi Derricotte

The Minks

In the backyard of our house on Norwood,
there were five hundred steel cages lined up,
each with a wooden box
roofed with tar paper;
inside, two stories, with straw
for a bed. Sometimes the minks would pace
back and forth wildly, looking for a way out;
or else they'd hide in their wooden houses, even when
we'd put the offering of raw horse meat on their trays, as if
they knew they were beautiful
and wanted to deprive us.
In spring the placid kits
drank with glazed eyes.
Sometimes the mothers would go mad
and snap their necks.
My uncle would lift the roof like a god
who might lift our roof, look down on us
and take us out to safety.
Sometimes one would escape.
He would go down on his hands and knees,
aiming a flashlight like
a bullet of light, hoping to catch
the orange gold of its eyes.
He wore huge boots, gloves
so thick their little teeth couldn't bite through.
"They're wild," he'd say. "Never trust them."
Each afternoon when I put the scoop of raw meat rich
with eggs and vitamins on their trays,
I'd call to each a greeting.
Their small thin faces would follow as if slightly curious.
In fall they went out in a van, returning
sorted, matched, their skins hanging down on huge metal
hangers, pinned by their mouths.
My uncle would take them out when company came
and drape them over his arm—the sweetest cargo.
He'd blow down the pelts softly
and the hairs would part for his breath
and show the shining underlife which, like

the shining of the soul, gives us each
character and beauty.

After a Reading at a Black College

Maybe one day we will have
written about this color thing
until we've solved it. Tonight
when I read my poems about
looking white, the audience strains
forward with their whole colored
bodies–a part of each person praying
that my poems will make sense.
Poems do that sometimes–take
the craziness and salvage some
small clear part of the soul,
and that is why, though frightened,
I don't stop the spirit. After,
though some people come
to speak to me, some
seem to step away,
as if I've hurt them once
too often and they have
no forgiveness left. I feel myself
hurry from person to person, begging.
Hold steady, Harriet Tubman whispers,
Don't flop around.
Oh my people,
sometimes you look at me
with such unwillingness–
As I look at *you!*
I keep trying to prove
I am not what I think you think.

For Black Women Who Are Afraid

A black woman comes up to me at break in the writing
workshop and reads me her poem, but she says she

can't read it out loud because
there's a woman in a car on her way
to work and her hair is blowing in the breeze
and, since her hair is blowing, the woman must be
white, and she shouldn't write about a white woman
whose hair is blowing, because
maybe the black poets will think she wants to be
that woman and be mad at her and say she hates herself,
and maybe they won't let her explain
that she grew up in a white neighborhood
and it's not her fault; it's just what she sees.
But she has to be so careful. I tell her to write
the poem about being afraid to write,
and we stand for a long time like that,
respecting each other's silence.

Everett Hoagland

From Ground Zero

. . . while the tale of how we suffer, . . . and
how we may triumph is never new, it always
must be heard . . . it's the only light we've got
in all this darkness . . .
–James Baldwin

Our thoughts and prayers rise to the jet
stream at *this* ground zero and drift
toward eternity like floating Japanese
memorial lanterns. At Ground Zero, USA,

hopefully, we shall come to see, to divine
what is holy, what is hateful, deep within
our private darknesses, when we gaze

up

at both wholly empty towering spaces,
edifices of air 2819 stories high.
Ground Zero: the post-Hiroshima point where

we, collectively,
as propheted nations
heavenward world,
ensouled species,
of profit-driven foreign policies,
O, so woefully, hit

bottom.

From here, by all that was,
by all who were
cruelly burned to crematory ash,
and in the name of all those

gone,

massacred, ground
down to irreducible dust,

mashed into hate-made mortar
of their first memorial,
the eternal day-after wreckage
in our mass
TV memory, the only way out of it

is up.
We must mine the motherlodes
of truth and light in our minds beyond
sorely cratered jingoism at Ground Zero,

to come to see, know, act as if
all air, water sources, lives are sacred,
all of earth is homeland, holy land, and
all of us blooded kin. Or how shall we

survive ourselves? We must
even more ". . . highly resolve . . ." that
for humanity
to *live more abundantly,*

there shall be no
inhumanity
in any nation's world
or domestic policies.
That again and again,
we humans must try
to be humane. Or we
will all go

down into the unlit pit,
the black hole of hate
at Ground Zero
into which so much
and so many—in different
times and places—have already

fallen.

How Could All That Have Happened Here?

> . . . by stealth, deceit, and murder . . .
> −From the National Day of Mourning speech by
> President George W. Bush
>
> . . . a case of "the chickens coming home to roost."
> −Malcolm X

by   the way cortez forcibly gold-filled
           the halls of montezuma
           to gild the church's cross-
           shaped sword

by   how the taino and carib were
           first ex'd by papal bull
           and councils of blood-rited cardinals
           for evermore
           land

by   maltreatment treaties
           righteously read aloud
           in portuguese spanish dutch french danish english
           to earth-toned native peoples who were
           done in by the dirty dozens
           in mines on reservations

by   a two
           hundred years yellowing
           white lie out of monticello titled
           the declaration

by   three-fifths-human middle passaged africans
           in the americas for four hundred years
           wholly taken peoples bought and sold
           by way of blessed slave ships
           from sea to shining sea
           and the shores of Tripoli

by   queen victoria's secrets
           about the sun never setting
           on covetous imperialism

by   africa cut up served
        up like a sun-yellow yam pie
        at the berlin conference

by   a century of harbored home-
        made every day american way terrorist groups
        like the kkk who enforce jim crow
        that sharecropped
        my fellow americans
        castrated for trophies while lynched
        for mason/dixon jars
        of preserved strange fruit
        in whiskey and rye
        any my my miss american thigh

TERRORISM IS AS AMERICAN AS BLACK
TESTICLE PIE

        served with stirred destablized chile
        and allende out-
        right ousted

by   our installations
        of pinochet and shah

by   our national security killings of kennedy's
        king lumumba cabral and all
        the others other than us
        in our immigration-based migrant working u.s.a.
        them-versus-us-american-way

by   recent stealth bombers

by   many thousand gone
        from our surgical airstrike over panama
        city in a country big stick teddy
        said he outright "took"

by   especially specious ways
        and mean means that legitimize
        whys and wherefores of appropriation

by   the historical red-white-and-black racism
        used to justify injustices
        in burned down rosewood and blacktown tulsa
        oklahoma and m.o.v.e.
        afrika on osage avenue
        west of brotherly love
        and the mississippi army camp van dorn massacre
        of over 1200 unarmed black american soldiers
        by white american soldiers by order
        of their officers one pre-my lai night
        during world war two

by   *craft and power that are great*
        and armed with cruel hate
        for all those niggerredskincolliewetbackcameljockey
        towelheadspicslantgooks gone
        for liberty and justice for all

by   way of "bombs away!"
        over:
        afghanistan (again)
        vieques
        yugoslavia
        afghanistan
        sudan
        iraq
        panama
        el salvador
        libya
        grenada
        guatemala
        cambodia
        vietnam
        laos
        peru
        congo
        cuba

by   boomerang jet wings

by   the vietnam war prolonged for
        industrial/military complex cash

and caches of cut off curled rind
yellow souvenir enemy ears for
"four more years"

by   globalization as in the hymn
"he's got the whole world in his hands"
by white lies about blacks browns yellows reds

by   imposing our/*his*
will be done
as neomanifest destiny
on palestinians just
as had been unjustly
done to/with american indians

by   all the peoples and land we have
put down used up bombed outright
taken
"by any means necessary"

Break
Time

Why don't you drink
your coffee with cream?
Why don't you use
sugar in your coffee?

I like purity where possible.
I am fond of facts and black coffee's
flavor. I like coffee and savor
Kenyan, Kona, Columbian,
blue-black Maroon Mountain.

Like our history, a lot of coffee
is already blended. Mixed like us
and the brutal truths
about us: invasion, rape, massacre, trans-

port, auction, forced labor, oppression, Empire
States, buildings, gold, sugar, cocoa, rum, rice,
cotton. Rebellion, spirituals, Jubilee, jazz, jive, over-
coming . . .

I like coffee-coffee not decaf,
not that chemically flavored stuff
in red, white and blue cans.
I like coffee with-
out cream-and-sugar (cattle barons, Indian Wars/
Barbados, Cuba, Haiti, Martinique.)

I like pure-D coffee,
you see; the dark roast beans
are brown navels. Sugar?

*S*ugar! *H*oney!! *I*ce *T*ea!!!

Sweetie, powdered sugar is scraped,
dead, black skin.
We were caned, processed like rum,
"refined," made molasses
colored. Our speech and values
distilled, refined like four-x powdered sugar.

The raging Age Of Reason's
blue stockings' sweet toothed
Enlightenment whitened us.
French Sun Kings' courts' confections
were party favors for titled, mannered
patrons of the art with powdered, painted
faces and long-haired wigs who would
pour baker's sugar all over a bought black
bon bon's sweaty body, lick it off, forcibly French
him or her to the point of exclamation, screaming

God's name, silently, with a cutout tongue,
or one stung dumb. Like anyone abducted,
operated on by aliens documented on the real
triple "X-Files" of skin tone
and off-color consciousness.

And if you think
that's something,
dig
the history of high
tea! Made an imperial institution
by an English Queen Bee
named after Victory. But the crown
jewel sun set on The Great Atlantic
and Pacific Tea company.

So
sip
and savor your history,
your coffee or your tea,
thoughtfully; it is an act
of communion with your ancestry:
negro, indio, wog, coolie, peon, overlord, over-

seer. And you will
see
shackled ghosts in
coffee's coffles;
taste
bandy-legged, black babies'
cane chew pacifiers,
the bittersweet sweat and blood
of slavery;
hear
the cane knives of up-
rising hacking away at hatred
to the bone, to the bone;

feel
the pulse of diasporic diabetes among
Bloods;
understand
the self-generating increases
of the triangular trade. Now

we are being canned.
and somewhere Over The Rainbow

of Third World Countries
neocolonials have reestablished
high tea's sterling silver service,
diamond-shaped scones, boney
black domestics and honey-tongued
bread-and-butter bosses. Their
inroads lead back to Cecil Rhodes.

Where is the fidelity?

Where are the stand-up folk
like Castro who committed,
50,000 Cubans who left
to fight for right in Portuguese
Africa? This nation's
capitol's capital is
resurrecting *Cuba Libra*
cocktails, casinos, prostitution:
entertainments for the wrongful
Right.

Where, wordsmiths,
in all our artfulness
is the new Truth, the Douglass, Wells,
DuBois, Malcolm, Fanon, Cabral, Nyerere????????
Superman was not
a 1930's cartoon character,
some American Way archangel
born out of The (Great?) Depression.

He was Paul Robeson
born out of a son of American slavery.
And *Here* . . . (We) . . . *Stand*
on his legacy and all that history
in our supremely paid for present
with no name but Junior
for what's about to be
a stillborn
future. Where
do/are you?? Are we
House Blends

really free? Truly
who and what we can be??

We shall see; we shall
see, hear, feel, understand and act
on the haunting, freeing facts.

*H*aki R. Madhubuti

Books as Answer

In recognition of National Black Book Week
(February 23–March 1)

there was only one book in our home
it was briefly read on sundays and
in between the lies & promises of smiling men
who slept with their palms out & pants unzipped.
it was known by us children as *the* sunday book.

rain and books & sun and books to read
in a home where books were as strange as
money and foreign policy discussions
and I alone searched for meaning
where rocks & belts & human storms
disguised themselves as answers, reference and revelation.
and I a young map of what is missing and wrong
in a home empty of books, void of liberating
words dancing as poetry and song,
vacuous of language that reveals pictures of
one's own fields, spirits, cities and defining ideas.
and I without the quiet contemplation that meditative prose
    demands,
was left free to drink from the garbage cans of riotous
    imaginations,
was sucked into the poverty of cultural destruction & violent
    answers.

until
someone, a stranger, a dark skinned woman with natural hair,
in a storefront library laid a book in front of me
and the language looked like me, walked like me,
talked to me, pulled me into its rhythms & stares,
slapped me warmly into its consciousness and read,
rain and books & sun and books,
we are each other's words & winds
we are each other's breath & smiles,
we are each other's memories & mores,
we build our stories page by page
chapter by chapter, poem by poem, & play by play

to create a life, family, culture, & a civilization
where it will take more than sixty seconds
to tell strangers who you really are,
to tell enemies and lovers your name.

The B Network

brothers bop & pop and be-bop in cities locked up
and chained insane by crack and other acts
of desperation computerized in pentagon cellars producing
boppin brothers boastin of being better, best & beautiful.

if the boppin brothers are beautiful where are the sisters
who seek brotherman with a drugless head unbossed or beaten
by the bodacious West?

in a time of big wind being blown by boastful brothers,
will other brothers beat back backwardness to better & best
without braggart bosses beatin butts,
takin names and diggin graves?

beatin badness into bad may be urban but is it beautiful &
    serious?
or is it betrayal in an era of prepared easy death hangin on
corners trappin young brothers before they know the
difference between big death and big life?

brothers bop & pop and be-bop in cities locked up
and chained insane by crack and other acts
of desperation computerized in pentagon cellars producing
boppin brothers boastin of being better, best, beautiful
and definitely not *Black.*

the critical best is that
brothers better be the best if they are to avoid backwardness
brothers better be the best if they are to conquer beautiful bigness
Comprehend that bad is only *bad* if it's big, Black and better
than boastful braggarts belittling our best and brightest
with bosses seeking inches when miles are better.

brothers need to bop to being Black & bright & above board
the black train of beautiful wisdom that is bending this bind
toward a new & knowledgeable beginning that is
bountiful & bountiful & beautiful
While be-boppin to be
better than the test,
brotherman.

better yet write the exam.

Mothers

For Mittie Travis (1897–1989), Maxine Graves Lee
(1924–1959), Inez Hall, and Gwendolyn Brooks

Mothers are not to be confused with females who only
birth babies

mountains have less height
and
elephants less weight than
mothers who plan bright futures for their children
against the sewers of western life.

mothers making magical music miles from monster madness
are not news,
are not subject for doctorates.

how shall we celebrate mothers?
how shall we call them in the winter of their lives?
what melody will cure slow bones?
who will bring them worriless late-years?
who will thank them for hidden pains?

mothers are not broken-homes,
they are irreplaceable fire,
a kiss or smile at a critical juncture,
a hug or reprimand when doubts swim in,
a calm glance when the world seems impossible,
the back that america could not break.

mothers making magical music miles from monster madness
are not news,
are not subject for doctorates.

mothers instill questions and common sense,
urge mighty thoughts and lively expectations,
are impetus for discipline and intelligent work while
making childhood exciting, unforgettable and challenging.

mothers are preventative medicine
they are
women who hold their children all night to break fevers,
women who cleaned other folks' homes in order to give their
    children one,
women who listen when others laugh,
women who believe in their children's dreams,
women who lick the bruises of their children and
give up their food as they suffer hunger pains silently.

if mothers depart their precious spaces too early
values, traditions and bonding interiors are wounded,
morals confused, ethics unknown, needed examples absent and
crippling histories of other people's victories are passed on as
    knowledge.

mothers are not broken-homes,
they are gifts
sharing full hearts, friendships and mysteries.
as the legs of fathers are amputated
mothers double their giving
having seen the deadly future of white flowers.

mothers making magical music miles from monster madness
are not news,
are not subject for doctorates.

who will bring them juice in the sunset of their time?
who will celebrate the wisdom of their lives,
the centrality of their songs,
the quietness of their love,
the greatness of their dance?

it must be us,
able daughters, good sons
their cultural gift,
the fruits and vegetables of their medicine.

We must come like earthrich waterfalls.

Bernice Johnson Reagon

Greed

For, a few years now,
I have been thinking about how to talk about greed

For a few years now,
I've been wondering if there was a way I could sing about greed

You see, in my opinion
Greed is at the heart of what's wrong with the world
At the very center of what is crippling about human society

Greed is a progressive viral-like disease,
with humankind twisted in its grip
Highly contagious
With a long incubation period of wanting and wishing

In the Beginning–
Greed expresses its presence in small increments
before springing forth in full bloom

It is want–
out of control, masquerading as need
And we in the U.S.A.
Are sinking in a mighty rampaging epidemic

From the very beginning
This thing greed has been with us
The peoples of England,
Pilgrims,
Puritans,
Quakers,
Colonizers who came to these shores
Came wanting more than freedom of spirit and mind and body

They wanted freedom to possess
Freedom to own
Not just enough to sustain
But to own as much as they could
Land–even people–even us

And there would never be an end to the
"As much as they could"
Never Never would there be Enough
Expansion became the word
First across the continent
Then starting over again
With the nearest farmlands
just outside of the city–
they became suburbs
And then to the farthest farmlands–
they became resorts
And now they have started to watch what they call
the Decaying inner cities
that's where we live
They say we are in need of a fix
They are positioning themselves

to

Start all over again
With the very cities they abandoned to create the suburbs.
To have more

Greed makes expansion a holy word
Ignoring that in nature,
Growth takes place within boundaries
When growth grows beyond boundaries
We have a name for it
We call it cancer

Or

The big C
It often leads to death
We treat it by trying to cut it out
But it sometimes–after the surgery–
The cells cool it
Hiding under the liver
And when the coast is clear
It leaps out again devouring everything in its path–Me, You, Us

The greed disease
Drives you with a hunger
There always has to be something else
To buy
To take
To control
To own
To win

The Greed disease is sneaky
Even while it is festering inside me
I feel secure in myself because I can see it so clearly in you
I can watch others there and see it clearly
Taking over
Over there

Greed's best defense is that it can
almost
Only be readily recognized
Diagnosed
In the eye of the beholder—
Turned on the beholder's neighbor

What looks like greed to me,
Is normal to the one upon whom I wish to place the label
I can see it clearly in me
We are blind to it in ourselves
And greed marches on

The greed disease created a philosophy of the righteousness of
    plenty
Possessing much more than enough,
Is proof of righteousness
You have so much because God has blessed you

And if you ain't got a lot
Well that is just evidence that you are wrong
You are a failure

The killing thing about this disease
Is that its contagion knows no bounds

Even as the founding fathers had it
The starving workers, slaves, and rented laborers—they got it
The middle class, they got it
Our kids with their correct sneakers,
and jackets,
and guns and knives—got it
The teachers, they got it
Me in my Kente cloth and Mud cloth, I got it

You cannot be in the culture and not have it
This having more than you need to sustain life-extending growth
I get it in the air I breathe
Every fiber of this land
Is permeated with it.
Our babies are born to it

But all need not be lost

There is that which offers the possibility of control
Inner control—watching my own self
Monitoring how I move
Between
What I need
And what I want
Minding my first mind
That tells me clearly
if—that is
I have not choked down my first mind
Muffled it with external voices driving me to consume
My own first mind
Tells me what my boundary is

And

I can die of old age inside my own skin
And leave you with yours

NOTE: When Joanne Gabbin asked me to do the keynote address for the Furious
Flower Conference, I was struggling with some hard questions about human be-
ings. What was it within our nature that made us develop cultures that had us, as a
major strand, accumulating more than we needed to maintain a balance with our-

selves and the environment? I had always learned that gluttony was a sin. It was not preached about a lot in the church I grew up in because so many of us in the pulpit and the pews evidenced major participation in the sin. At the time I wrote this prose poem, greed surfaced in my mind as one of the major reasons human-generated cultures threatened the survival of the planet. I found myself talking not only about obvious huge examples–corporate, state, and institutional greed and destruction–but I also put myself to task. This piece continues to reorganize my life.

They Are All Falling around Me

They are falling all around me
They are falling all around me
They are falling all around me
The strongest leaves of my tree

Every paper bring the news that
Every paper bring the news that
Every paper bring the news that
The teachers of my sound are moving on

Death comes and rest so heavy
Death comes and rest so heavy
Death comes and rest so heavy
Your face I'll never see no more

But you're not really going to leave me
But you're not really going to leave me
But you're not really going to leave me

It is your path I walk
It is your song I sing
It is your air I breathe
It's the record you set that makes me go on
It's your strength that helps me stand
You're not really going to leave me

I will try to sing my song right
I will try to sing my song right
I will try to sing my song right
Be sure to let me hear from you

NOTE: The words of this song came to me early one morning when I had just gotten the news that another musician, from whom I had learned a lot, had died. In tears, I wrote this song out of a feeling of being uncovered. There is a comfort you have as a student when your teachers are still there to check and nurture you, but I got up that morning feeling a bit disoriented. It was as if–the teachers, the carriers of our singing traditions–their dying was a test for me. And now I would really have to find out if I had learned the lessons. As I acknowledged their moving on, I reached back to a memory from my childhood in Georgia when my father taught us that the dead are not dead. Sometimes this was not a comfortable or desired thing because there were those who die and are unready, or they are not properly assisted by the living to transition to the other side and they hang around. My father would say to my mother, "Dear, haunts riding those children." Then he would tell my mother what she would need to do. I could never figure out how he would know, but he was always right. We were taught that if you were sleeping and you came out of the sleep fighting to get your breath it was because you were being ridden by a haunt, the restless dead. So using that troubling personal reference as my gateway, I reached through to that place I've been taught about where the dead are not dead and asked them to continue to come to me. And this song is also grounded by the poem "Breaths" written by the Senegalese poet Birago Diop. Diop's poem, one of my favorites, celebrates that space in our universe where the dead continues to be with us if we are open to receive.

$\mathcal{N}$ikki Giovanni

The Wrong Kitchen

Grandmother would sit me
between her legs
to scratch my dandruff
and unravel my plaits

We didn't know then
dandruff was a sign of nervousness
hives tough emotional decisions
things seen that were better
unseen

We thought love could cure
anything a doll here a favorite
caramel cake there

The arguments the slaps the chairs
banging against the wall
the pleas to please stop
would disappear under quilts aired
in fresh air
would be forgotten after Sunday School
teas and presentations for the Book Club

We didn't know then why I played
my radio all night
and why I kept a light burning

We thought back then it was my hair
that was nappy

So we—trying to make it all right—
straightened the wrong kitchen

Legacies

her grandmother called her from the playground
   "yes, ma'am" said the little girl

"i want chu to learn how to make rolls" said the old
woman proudly
but the little girl didn't want
to learn how because she knew
even if she couldn't say it that
that would mean when the old one died she would be less
dependent on her spirit so
the little girl said
"i don't want to know how to make no rolls"
with her lips poked out
and the old woman wiped her hands on
her apron saying "lord
these children"
and neither of them ever
said what they meant
and i guess nobody ever does

Nikki-Rosa

childhood remembrances are always a drag
if you're Black
you always remember things like living in Woodlawn
with no inside toilet
and if you become famous or something
they never talk about how happy you were to have
your mother
all to yourself and
how good the water felt when you got your bath
from one of those
big tubs that folk in chicago barbecue in
and somehow when you talk about home
it never gets across how much you
understood their feelings
as the whole family attended meetings about Hollydale
and even though you remember
your biographers never understand
your father's pain as he sells his stock
and another dream goes
And though you're poor it isn't poverty that

concerns you
and though they fought a lot
it isn't your father's drinking that makes any difference
but only that everybody is together and you
and your sister have happy birthdays and very good
Christmasses
and I really hope no white person ever has cause
to write about me
because they never understand
Black love is Black wealth and they'll
probably talk about my hard childhood
and never understand that
all the while I was quite happy

Jerry W. Ward Jr.

I Have Felt the Gulf: Mississippi

I have felt the Gulf churn butter
and fish ignore with beautiful indifference
the fatal harmony of salt and oilwater.
Turtles, housed in theory, laugh.
Veracity, audacious and violent, rises
as wrecked richness to surface
and ride raveling waves to
shore: beach, a long breadbrown
slice of careless nature, awaits
this gift, miracle spread,
as if, perhaps, then again, maybe, why
my boat-tossed face was hushed
to utter awe at the ceiling
of language, a storm-verbed sky.

Journey 55

song in arrivals

You survive the surreal
path through trees who
weep as brooms complain
of being misused as instruments
of a slave-jumping point.

Owls fear your power.
Lions roar your praise.

Such wonders on the star/trail
inspire the utterance
of a child's clean mouth:
the truly hip do not hop
with rabbits' abandon.
They dance designs.

Your light/love speaks
critique in dialogue

with desires unchained.
Your metaphor's revealed.

Time remarks thus:
law would order the spine
be broken at the brainbase.

You escape, leave no ashes.
The lynched phoenix salutes
your legend.

Memory smiles.
Only wind will call your name.

Bells inscribe
your dying
to live
the balance
beautiful.

After the Report from Iron Mountain

Lies are as at home
in the traps of Venus
as they are

           in the three-edged blade
           the bullet opening my enemy
           whose voice is a flute
           bleating in the Asian sun:
           I hear no conflict of interest
           in the groan of death

           For it is evident
           soldiers are hard,
           even in today's world
           where salt-free resolution
           is assigned a priority of social value

Tragedy. Anyhow
tragedy's a goat song
of words that will not play.
Anyhow, who gives a damn.
We left Viet Nam

>and a trail of blood, intestines, Agent
>Orange trees. The boatpeople followed,
>real imaginary, they spawned
>and pawned and came half-raped,
>half-maimed upon
>the pirate-mined South China Sea,
>to drown like Haitians
>that cannot be dissolved
>in Florida's whimsy-driven waters,
>that cannot be resolved
>without bartering, cheapening war.

For it is evident
that even in today's world
there exists no priority of social value,
real or imaginary,
between citizens and modest molecules.
There exists no interest,
real or imaginary.

After the report
influence accepts no boundaries
like the Chilean poet
who found no conflict of interest
in playing guitar without fingers.

After all, it was only a sound
the world wanted,
the crackle of *newsprint,*
the dying toi-toi of hair in Soweto.

>If resolution were assigned
>a priority of social value
>we'd blind ourselves
>to see better

In the blackness of being
an Arab-Catholic-Jew
I taste weeping in Beirut,
savor the colonial afterbirth
of holocaust in a mosque
crack my teeth upon the illusion
prepared on the table before me
as in a bazaar of women and children
abused to nothing
real or imaginary.

        I walk the valley
        between the social forces
        of nations, oblivious to evil,
        for my ghetto blaster
        offers comfort.

Tragedy. Anyhow
who gives a damn.
Neither man nor memory
finds a conceivable conflict of interest,
real or imaginary,
in the acid rain between nations,
that cannot be resolved in recourse to war.
Anyhow, who gives a damn.

Tragedy's just an old goat
song of interest,
real or imaginary,
between me and the words
and the paraclete birds whispering revelations
in amber waves of grain: enemies turn eternal
in the black holes of the sun.

Lorenzo Thomas

Dangerous Doubts

The mind invents its own inadequacies
But not the power to erase illusion
That schemes and wholesome dreams
Can become actual despite the truth
That thoughts invest themselves in flesh
And direct motion

That you have 30,000 shots at immortality
But only one you dare not miss at being rich
Or at the least escape the nag of destitution

That maybe exercise shows on TV
Are really harmful
That sound bodies just
Amplify our empty minds

That platitudes contain a grain of wisdom
And fortune's a rush hour train that doesn't wait

To really live means needing other people
That whatever that means love
Could conquer hate

L'Argent

I know you don't know what
Love is it isn't
Dagwood kisses on the way to work
It's going to work

Love could be but it's not
A 50/50 partnership
Matched sets of polished lies
A usury of affection

I understand that you don't understand
Money don't grow on trees

And if it did,
Those trees would grow
So far away
It would be work to get it

Back in the Day

When we were boys
We called each other "Man"
With a long *n*
Pronounced as if a promise

We wore felt hats
That took a month to buy
In small installments
Shiny Florsheim or Stacey Adams shoes
Carried our dancing gait
And flashed our challenge

Breathing our aspirations into words
We harmonized our yearnings to the night
And when old folks on porches dared complain
We cussed them out
                              under our breaths
And walked away
                    And once a block away
Held learned speculations
About the character of their relations
With their mothers

It's true
That every now and then
We killed each other
Borrowed a stranger's car
Burned down a house
But most boys went to jail
For knocking up a girl
He really   truly   deeply   loved
            really   truly   deeply

But was too young
Too stupid, poor, or scared
To marry

Since then I've learned
Some things don't never change:
The breakfast chatter of the newly met
Our disappointment
With the world as given

Today,
News and amusements
Filled with automatic fire
Misspelled alarms
Sullen posturings and bellowed anthems
Our scholars say
Young people doubt tomorrow

This afternoon I watched
A group of young men
Or tall boys
Handsome and shining with the strength of futures
Africa's stubborn present
To a declining white man's land
Lamenting
As boys always did and do
Time be moving on
Some things don't never change
And how
               back in the day
Well
               things were somehow better

They laughed and jived
Slapped hands
And called each other "Dog"

Yusef Komunyakaa

Songs for My Father

I told my brothers I heard
You & mother making love,
Your low moans like a blues
Bringing them into the world.
I didn't know if you were laughing
Or crying. I held each one down
& whispered your song in their ears.
Sometimes I think they're still jealous
Of our closeness, having forgotten
We had to square-off & face each other,
My fists balled & cocked by haymakers.
That spring I lifted as many crossties
As you. They can't believe I can
Remember when you had a boy's voice.

*

You were a quiet man
Who'd laugh like a hyena
On a hill, with your head
Thrown back, gazing up at the sky.
But most times you just worked
Hard, rooted in the day's anger
Till you'd explode. We always
Walked circles around
You, wider each year,
Hungering for stories
To save us from ourselves.
Like a wife who isn't touched,
We had to do something bad
Before you'd look into our eyes.

*

We spent the night before Easter
Coloring eggs & piling them into pyramids
In two crystal punch bowls.
Our suits, ties, white shirts, shoes,
All lined up for the next day.
We had memorized our passages

From the bible, about the tomb
& the angel rolling back the stone.
You were up before daybreak,
In the sagebush, out among goldenrod
& mustard weed, hiding the eggs
In gopher holes & underneath roots.
Mother always argued with you,
Wondering why you made everything so hard.

*

We stood on a wooden platform
Facing each other with sledgehammers,
A copper-tipped sieve sunken into the ground
Like a spear, as we threaded on five foot
Of galvanized pipe for the pump.
As if tuned to some internal drum,
We hammered the block of oak
Placed on top of the pipe.
It began inching downward
As we traded blows–one for you,
One for me. After a half hour
We threaded on another five foot. The sweat
Gleamed on our shirtless bodies, father
& son tied to each other till we hit water.

*

Goddamn you. Goddamn you.
If you hit her again, I'll sail through
That house like a dustdevil.
Everyone & everything here
Is turning against you,
That's why I had to tie the dog
To a tree before you could chastise us.
He darted like lightning through the screen door.
I know you'll try to kill me
When it happens. You know
I'm your son & it's bound to happen.
Sometimes I close my eyes till I am
On a sea of falling dogwood blossoms,
But someday this won't work.

*

I confess. I am the ringleader
Who sneaked planks out of the toolshed,
Sawed & hammered together the wagon.
But I wasn't fool enough to believe
That you would've loved our work.
So, my brothers & I dug a grave
In the corner of the field for our wagon
That ran smooth as a Nat King Cole
Love ballad. We'd pull it around
The edge of our world & rebury it
Before the 5 o'clock mill whistle blew.
I bet it's still there, the wood gray
& light as the ribs of my dog Red
After somebody gunned him down one night

*

You banged a crooked nail
Into a pine slab,
Wanting me to believe
I shouldn't have been born
With hands & feet
If I didn't do
Your kind of work.
You hated my books.
Sometimes at dusk,
I faced you like that
Childhood friend you trained
Your heart to always run
Against, the horizon crimson
As the eyes of a fighting cock.

*

I never asked how you
Passed the driver's test,
Since you could only write
& read your name. But hell,
You were good with numbers;
Always counting your loot.
That Chevy truck swerved

Along back roads night & day.
I watched you use wire
& sunlight to train
The stongest limbs,
How your tongue never obeyed
The foreman, how the truck motor
Was stunted, frozen at sixty.

*

You wanted to fight
When I told you that a woman
Can get rid of a man
With a flake of lye
In his bread each day.
When you told her what I said
I bet the two of you made love
Till the thought flew out of your head.
Now, when you stand wax-faced
At the door, your eyes begging
Questions as you mouth wordless
Songs like a red-belly perch,
Assaying the scene for what it is,
I doubt if love can part my lips.

*

Sometimes you could be
That man on a red bicycle,
With me on the handlebars,
Just rolling along a country road
On the edge of July, honeysuckle
Lit with mosquito hawks.
We rode from under the shady
Overhang, back into sunlight.
The day bounced off car hoods
As the heat & stinking exhaust
Brushed against us like a dragon's
Roar, nudging the bike with a tremor,
But you steered us through the flowering
Dogwood like a thread of blood.

*

You lean on a yard rake
As dry leaves & grass smolder
In a ditch in mid March,
Two weeks before your sixty-first
Birthday. You say I look happy,
I must be in love. It is 1986,
Five months before your death.
You toss a stone at the two dogs
Hooked together in a corner of the yard.
You smile, look into my eyes
& say you want me to write you a poem.
I stammer for words. You
Toss another stone at the dogs
& resume raking the leafless grass.

*

I never said thanks for Butch,
The wooden dog you pulled by a string.
It was ugly as a baldheaded doll.
Patched with wire & carpenter's glue, something
I didn't believe you had ever loved.
I am sorry for breaking it in half.
I never meant to make you go
Stand under the falling snowflakes
With your head bowed on Christmas
Day. I couldn't look at Butch
& see that your grandmother Julia,
The old slave woman who beat you
As if that's all she knew, had put love
Into it when she carved the dog from oak.

*

I am unlike Kikuji
In Kawabata's *Thousand Cranes,*
Since I sought out one of your lovers
Before you were dead.
Though years had passed
& you were with someone else,
She thought I reminded her

Of a man she'd once known.
She pocketed the three dollars.
A big red lampshade bloodied
The room, as if held by a mad
Diogenes. Yes, she cried out,
But she didn't sing your name
When I planted myself in her.

*

You spoke with your eyes
Last time I saw you, cramped
Between a new wife & the wall. You couldn't
Recognize funeral dirt stamped down
With dancesteps. Your name & features half
X-ed out. I could see your sex,
Your shame, a gold-toothed pout,
As you made plans for the next house you'd build,
Determined to prove me wrong. I never knew
We looked so much like each other. Before
I could say I loved you, you began talking money,
Teasing your will with a cure in Mexico.
You were skinny, bony, but strong enough to try
Swaggering through that celestial door.

Kalamu ya Salaam

Sharing is hereditary

my four foot-eleven mother was world wise yet unburdened
by the cloying cynicism sophistication so often suggests
she projected a generous spirit adeptly balancing gifting
and keeping her nose out of other people's greed, and
equally, my burly country bred father taught us
the eternal lesson: regardless of how you looked
or what others thought, there was no wrong in doing right

the curatorial joy of their prescient caring shaped three
strapping sons who continue to strive to match inola's
exalted social statue and to embody big val's prophetic
folk wisdom, our parents offered the treasury of themselves
and thereby ushered our entrance into the sanctuary
of responsive and responsible manhood wherein we fulfill
ourselves by emptying our hearts into the life cups of others

The Call of the Wild

Poetry is not an answer
Poetry is a calling
       a vision that does not vanish
       just because nothing
       concrete comes along or
       because the kingdom of heaven
       is under some tyrant's foot

Poetry is not a right
Poetry is a demand
       to be left alone
       or joined together or whatever
       we need to live

Poetry is not an ideology
       poets choose life
       over ideas, love people
       more than theories, and really would
       prefer a kiss to a lecture.

Poetry

Poetry is not a government
Poetry is a revolution
        guerillas–si!
        politicians–no!

Poetry is always hungry
        for all that is
        forbidden
        poetry never stops drinking
        not even after the last drop, if we
        run out of wine poets will
        figure a way to ferment rain

Poetry wears taboos
        like perfume with a red shirt
        and a feather in the cap
        sandals or bare feet, and
        sleeps nude with the door unlocked

Poetry cuts up propriety into campfire logs and sits
        around proclaiming life's glories far into
        each starry night
Poetry burns prudence
        like it was a stick of aromatic incense or
        revels in becoming
        the even more fragrant odor of the heretic
        aflame at the stake, eternally unwilling
        to swear allegiance
        to foul-breathed censors
        with torches in their hands

Poetry smells like a fart
        in every single court of law and smells
        like fresh mountain air
        in every dank jail cell

Poetry is unreliable

Poetry will always jump the fence
>   just when you think poets are behind you
>   they show up somewhere off the beaten path
>   absent without leave, beckoning for you
>   to take your boots off and listen to the birds

Poetry is myopic and refuses to wear glasses
>   never sees no trespassing signs and always
>   prefers to be up touching close to everything
>   skin to skin, skin to sky, skin to light
>   poetry loves skin, loathes coverings

Poetry is not mature
>   it will act like a child
>   to the point of social embarrassment
>   if you try to pin poetry down
>   it will throw a fit
>   yet it can sit quietly for hours
>   playing with a flower

Poetry has no manners
>   it will undress in public everyday of the week
>   go shamelessly naked at high noon on holidays
>   and play with itself, smiling

Poetry is not just sexual
>   not just monosexual
>   nor just homosexual
>   nor just heterosexual
>   nor bisexual
>   or asexual
>   poetry is erotic and is willing
>   any way you want to try it

Poetry

Poetry has no god
>   there is no church of poetry
>   no ministers and certainly no priests
>   no catechisms nor sacred texts
>   and no devils either

or sin, for that matter, original
synthetic, cloned or otherwise, no sin

Poetry

in the beginning was the word
and from then until the end
let there always be

Poetry!

Directions for Understanding Modern Jazz Criticism

dedicated to gail syphax who peeped this a long time ago

1. Get A Blank
    White
    Sheet
    Of Paper

2. Draw A Box
    (Size Does Not Matter)

3. Look Inside
    The Box

4. Notice The Color
    And Significance Of Everything
    Inside Your Lines

5. You Now Understand
    The Vast Majority Of Jazz Criticism

Dorothy Marie Rice

Taproots

October: no frost,
yet.
She rakes sugar maple
leaves,
a space for pansies;
Chops, with rusty hoe,
the ground: layered
rocks,
yellow clay; gnats
drift;
earthworms unravel;
She kneels;
breathes earth.
With bare fingers,
she pats
the ground;
tastes the
black soil;
On this occasion
Pansies speak:
Grandmother kneels
on hardscrabble soil,
digs
sweet potatoes.
Spirits
rise.

Ambrosia

*For: Gwendolyn Brooks, Joanne Gabbin,
and the Poetic Energy of Furious Flower*

Hush! Somebody's calling your name;
The first buzz you hear, tiny as a raindrop:
is our scout.

She wings
through ozone-drenched currents;
over asphalt highways,

Past bald-headed boys shooting
basketballs,
pot-bellied girls souring in their prime
new babies on their hips;

Past weary grandmothers who wonder
if a change will ever come.

Sturdy wings pumping through
miles, and miles, and miles . . .

Finally, a field of Timothy and Clover;
She rests;
tongues the purple sweetness;
baptizes herself in nectar;

Her dance
a figure-eight in midair:
Children,
go where I send thee . . .

We swarm:
a black cloud reshaping the horizon;
We nestle in the bosom
of mountains.

Remains

The odor of pine hangs heavy this morning. Last night
I heard the crack of limb, the snap of branches abrupt,
futile as a lamb's cry. It might have been lightning at first,
or old age weakening your top branches; and then
woodpeckers began their pneumatic drilling; yet,
you remained standing, springing with new life; dancing,
cavorting with the wind; bending under snow and ice,
then bouncing back: a haven for gray squirrels and blue jays.
Majestic.
This morning, ice-coated branches lie, on the frozen ground,
like broken bones.

Lamont B. Steptoe

Spookism

For Amiri Baraka and Ishmael Reed

i
been runnin' wid
spirits and spooks
all my life
why you think i'm still here?
i'm
the hipster hoodoo voodoo
warrior
of vibes and images
i dream liberation
and oppressors go mad!
you might see me anywhere
playing the blues under a streetlight
on the boulevard of oblivion
i got wings on my heels
i'm the junkyard dog
of the cosmos
the bagman of paradise
i carry time like dice
and nothin' smaller than a whirlwind
i
been runnin' wid
spirits and spooks
all my life
my eyes glow green dreams
words are wands
and I'm a goddamn Magician!
look me up
in the encyclopedia of SPOOKISM!

Contraband

invisible cargo arrived
with African captives
ship captains couldn't explain

why the boats rode
so low in the water
was it some dark giant
the color of the wind?
maybe
it was just the rhythm
hidden like diamonds in the bones
maybe
it was the dreams
in the sack of the heart
maybe
it was burning embers of rage
hidden beneath the tongue

Coming Ashore

For LaMer

she
never was
no baby
even when she
was seal slick
with her Momma's
blood
she
was born an old woman
disguised as infant
now
in the body of child
she be wild
free
she old as a discovered Mummy
in the valley of the Queens
she old
as lightnin'
and her speech
is the tide
coming ashore

Quo Vadis Gex-Breaux

Jazz Rain

She had a kind of classy coarseness
like raw silk
a kind of open earthiness
without being dirt
a way of saying things
that made them seem something
more than she meant
(sometimes a little less)

She moved with the breezes
without being flighty
capturing men's hearts
before they realized surrender
also meant their minds

She grew up with water sounds
split splat splat
on tin roofs
soft tappings on bare windowpanes
tip tip tip
after heavy cloudbursts

Rooms where she had been
danced alone and empty for hours
after she left
replaying her laughter
that fell like jazz rain
a slow, smooth, syncopated harmony
bursting later in thunderous
improvisational splendor
intricately weaving patterns
from rainbowed puddles in her head

Choice few could hear her music
read the notes to which she danced
hers was too cloistered an intellect
to teach steps meant only for select
who knew how to scat between life's drops

plish, plish, plish
do wa-a-a-a-a-a-a

Solo she sang her own harmonies
overdubbed and lightning sparkled
simply percussioned, softly strung
with wind-whistling horns
she glistened, spontaneous, evolving
defined by blues bridges
a wet, unfinished song.

Padded Steps/Sister Song (a litany)

Walk softly, my sister,

>   beauty, myth, legend
>   close to extinction. Yours
>   is the road too steep to
>   lose foot on lest it sink you
>   into eternal depths.

Walk softly,

>   gazelle remade daily
>   in your ancestors' images.
>   Picking cane and cotton.
>   Softly—maybe light steps will
>   leave less of a scent
>   to be tracked. But history
>   will insist that you be
>   hunted down in the bush
>   of your invented realities
>   those dreams you shared
>   and made real so that others
>   would have a path to

Walk softly, my sister.

>   Up in the middle of the night
>   rocking yours or somebody

else's baby. Soothing
someone's momentarily lost
soul. Carrying shadows
into swamp-pathed freedom

Walk softly, sister,

raising children, fruit
of man you "just wanted
to take care of." Your instincts
nurture growth. Softly–
crow reborn from human bones.
Phoenix rising out of hatred's ashes.
Form beyond definition.
Giver to a taking world.

Walk softly, sister.

Lifetimes are relative,
sometimes a hundred
years lived in twenty or
not even thirty lived
in ninety.

Walk softly, sister.

The drummer with
no sticks makes
you dance while others
hear no music. Softly–
play the piano as if
you read composers' spirits
not music on flat pages.

Walk softly, sister.

Sing your song, blue,
spiritual or sassy New
Orleans style, accompanied
by holy horns, sacred strings,
divine drums. Sing your

song, or play it out on
the river-front to waters
deep with buried wishes
sung daily by the waves.
Let the river's muddy deeps
heal raw middle passage scars
pried open daily by hopes snuffed
out by years of unrequited
yearning.

Walk softly, sister,

cooking and pouring
libation at foreign altars
while praying your way
through tomorrows torn
away from emptinesses that
wait hungrily at locked
mind-doors. The stars
the moon in its fullness
every dreary or blue
cloud bright day are yours
as your magic bounces off
mountains in monotonous minds.

Walk softly,

in your multi-hued finery
accented by a thousand
dialected tongues that
garden-scented ears hear.
Softly—talk to each other
mother to daughter, sister
to sister, aunt to niece, one
to another. Listen. And
let the words save you.

Walk softly, my sister.

Do not be consumed
by your longing and

remember to save some
of you for yourself.

Wisdom Is

For Tom

I see you Mama Goldie, Perdido
Street sage in tans and browns,
offering all the wisdom
you can gather from the
gray matter beneath your ever-
present head-rag.
More than neighbor and not
mom, you held my soul in
your heart where you fashioned
gifts beyond hand-holding advice.

Don't you worry 'bout nothin honey.
God don't like ugly. That woman's
gon get hers. And you don't have to be
the one givin it, you comforted
when I cried about my mean aunt
who sent me to school with liverwurst
sandwiches everyday, implied my hair
wasn't "good" enough and said I broke
my own bank when her spoiled son
took my savings.

Mama Goldie, you spread
your ancient arms wide,
hugged me in the broad
bosom of unconditional love,
knew I didn't lie, even if they
were the adults. You gave me
candy when I cried and said, *Girl,*
you're gon be somebody. You're
gon show 'em. They gonna be sorry
they didn't try to know you better.

I sleep a different
dream now and hunger for
someones to hold my
sons in their hearts. I still
lick wounds that neither
hurt less nor heal any sooner
than they did at ten. And
I hold fast to the memories
shaping them into prayer
as I conjure you Mama Goldie.

Memory Waves

Smelly Gulf water waves beckon
distant signals for lapping reminiscence
to float in on. Memories of home
are like that–pieces of wholes
half washed away messages
written before the tides came in.

I remember things my mother said
Our sitting around the table
the way she, by mood
burst into song so moving
that as a young child, I looked
for corners to sit in and sob
but I cannot hear her voice.

Oh my man I love him so
he'll never know. When
he takes me in his arms . . .
She sang the popular fare of her day.

I can remember how I felt
when she hugged me anyway
in my *don't want to be*
touched adolescence, the prescient
wisdom she freely shared
how I sometimes made her cry

and how she died before her
grandchildren were born just as
her mother before her
but I long to hear her again.

I listen to this voice that's mine
disappointed at its flat, non-
resonating timbre, and wonder.
But it is only a part—not whole.

I long for comforting sound
that conjures the familiar
like the scent of bread baking or
an unconditional embrace and
I long for sound. Clear
crisp, soprano, fluid sound
singing in the hollows of my soul,
my mother's voice.

É. Ethelbert Miller

Roy Campanella: January, 1958

Night as dark as the inside
of a catcher's mitt
There are blows I can take
head on and never step back
from. When Jackie made the news
I knew I would have a chance
to play ball in the majors.
Ten years ago I put the number
39 on my back and tonight God
tries to steal home.

Bringing Back the Draft

I suck your breasts
till your nipples
stand erect like two
small soldiers ready
to go to war

Whispers, Secrets, and Promises

afternoon
and your eyes walk
across the table into
my hands

this is the beginning
of confessions and faith
or how you braid your
hair

a metaphor
for things left
unsaid

*M*ona Lisa Saloy

The "N" Word

For Carolyn M. Rodgers

We all say it,
But we're not supposed to anymore.
There's the daily
"Who'd you call a nigger?" Or,
"Only niggers talk like that!"

They tell me,
I shouldn't use the "N" word in the new millennium,
In my poems, in hushed raps to a lover in the dark,
Or in any talk I might give.

They say the "N" word is a hold back
To Jim Crow times they'd rather
Forget, so not mentioning it
Eases the "N" word from memory.
Besides, it's disrespectful, vile, like the do do of our history.
And, we've come up to hyphenated status with
Origin of great pharaohs and queens,
That the "N" word is no
Longer relevant to our tomorrows.

So I say that I only call a nigger
A nigger when appropriate,
Such as in the case of dumb niggers, mean niggers,
Lucky niggers, big-leg niggers and big-butt niggers,
Fat niggers, big-lipped, and no-lipped niggers,
Kinky-hair niggers, and good-hair niggers,
Kiss-ass niggers, and kick-your-ass niggers,
Controversial niggers, famous niggers,
Has-been niggers, movie-star niggers,
Ball-playing, beer-drinking, coke-sniffing niggers,
Skinny, dread-locked niggers, and vegetarian niggers.

Grease-monkey niggers, and
Cowboy niggers on horses in Texas and Oakland, California,
Northern niggers who think they ain't niggers,
Beatnik niggers, hippy niggers,

Blues-singing, Jazz-bopping niggers, and
Rhythm-and-blues swinging niggers, and
Hip-hop, baggy-butt-pants niggers,
And we all know at least two sorry-assed niggers—
Niggers with a handful of gimme
And a mouthful of much obliged—
Important niggers and niggers who think they're important,
Ugly niggers that'll make a jailbird run free,
Pretty niggas that'll make the sun sit on a tree,
Old, corny, jive niggers with their:
 "What's the word?"
 "Thunderbird!"
 "What's the price?"
 "Thirty twice!"
There's neo-jive, mono-syllabic niggers with their "Word!"
Wise niggers like Oneida—a die-hard nationalist nigger—
Who says:
 "Niggers and flies
 I do despise.
 The more I see niggers,
 The more I like flies."
Canceling the "N" word is like throwing out the baby
When her clothes don't fit.
We're not speaking of nice Colored men, but
Trifling niggers without a pot to piss in,
No-count, nosey niggers—
Who mind your business and mine—
Brick-head red niggers, and Jungle-fever niggers.
This ain't no
 ennie-meanie-mini-mo flack.

This is niggerness and
Nigger raps for Doctor niggers
And teacher niggers and
Good niggers.
You know,
If they've got you've got niggers.
Real, down-to-the-ground,
Slap-it-on-your-thighs-and-laugh niggers,
Bones-playing niggers,
Street-smart niggers,

And mysterious-come-alive-after-five niggers,
Those midnight-rambler, all-night gambler niggers,
Sweet niggers, and naturally blue-black, brown, yellow niggers,
And uppity niggers.

I've got a neighbor,
A bonafide, high-yellow tenth generation
Creole nigger.
Says she's
Not Black, or a Negro.
She is Colored.
That's what it says on
Her birth certificate.
My colored neighbor hates sorry-assed,
Incompetent niggers.
Says she "don't want nothin' to do
With anything Black."
She won't call no
Nigger plumber,
No nigger electrician,
No nigger carpenter, 'cept family.
Only thing a nigger can do for her
Is get out of her way or die.
But worse she says is oreo niggers,
luke-warm niggers, and
Bougeoise niggers with their
Gucci, pucci, nike, air, pump, BMW,
Or Merced niggers.
You can bleach your skin.
You can texturize your hair.
You can eat crawfish with a fork,
but you're still a nigger, my nigger.

You're my nigger, if you don't get no bigger.
And, if you do get bigger, you'll be
My bigger nigger!

"Where y'at my nigger?
You're my main nigger,
My favorite turd,
And that ain't no shit!"

Hey my nigger.
You know, you're my nigger—
My nerve, my jelly preserve.

And for folks who talk about
        people like me,
        people my color (yellow),
They say
I don't know my identity
By the biological thinness of melanin.
First of all,
All niggers only been a nigger
A few times in their lives,
And I'm happy to say that
I'll only be a nigger
Six times in my life:
        a nigger baby
        a nigger girl
        a nigger woman.
Though I was a crippled nigger,
And I am a good nigger,
But one day I'll be a dead nigger.

   So, I hope that no card-carrying
African American, or no stamped, certified,
Colored, or Negro is ever insulted
Cause I call a nigger **my nigger.**

   Nigger please!

This Poem Is for You, My Sister

For Barbara Ann

Still eight years my elder
I remember clutching
your circular felt skirt,
me, all snotty-nosed and wanting
your rhinestone sweater.

I remember wishing
to follow you to the zoo
or the record shop
and being told to skip rope
or dream little Black girl dreams
of Saints, Voodoo Queens, or Guardian Angels.
But you fed me Brooke Benton,
Dinah Washington, and Ella Fitzgerald
as appetizers.
At 10, I was drunk on Nat King Cole,
Coltrane, and Miles Davis,
and my spirit would
never be measured in years again.

One fall, you ran from jim crow,
left for Seattle,
our room full of your rose hips sachets,
your old green leather jacket,
and the straight skirts I had no hips to fill.
My life, shaken without you,
was empty like a finished Barqs root beer.
I wore loneliness like
your hand-me-down skirts.
When the record player screeched,
I heard your voice—hey girl—
between Johnny Mathis melodies:
       "When Sunni gets blue
       She breathes a sigh of sadness
       Like the wind that stirs the tress. . . ."
Your face faint, floods me
with your Tchoupitoulas smile,
thick black braids,
never aging in your high-school photo.

After mother passed,
and brother joined the Marines,
and Daddy drank his memories sour
and stale as day-old beer breath,
I wanted you to answer my anger,
to wipe my tears dry

with a sock hop or
a backyard barbecue.

So I followed your memory
northwest, over Cascade mountains
and Suquamish tribes.
I heard mother's voice:
      "You mind good now ya hear.
      You mind your sister good, now."

You, mother of a son,
wife to a man
who believes love
an unidentified emotion,
tenderness, a foreign conspiracy.
Each season of mail
a burden like horror,
the hell on his shoulders
leaning on you like a sawhorse.
Your hands are
the color of gentleness and pacific sand,
your breasts broken with years
of curses cold as frostbite, and
our prayers melting each scream like fudge.
So sister love
dipped in golden seal
mouthfuls of carrot juice and holy water
broke the pain of those years
like a finger snap or a joke.

This poem is for you my sister
with your Tchoupitoulas smile,
your jet black braids,
that round bottom like mother's,
and your ankles that swell with the rain.

Still eight years my senior,
time peels away
Kiwi fruit memories
with seeds sprouting friendship
and globetrotting;

and as we skip across
Caribbean beaches or Pacific shores,
we swim among warm crowds.
Your eyes soothe me
like the Guardian Angel of my childhood dreams.
We are masked in love
and mother's smile.

This poem is for you my sister
with your Tchoupitoulas smile,
your jet black braids,
that round bottom like mother's,
and your ankles that swell with the rain.

We've Come This Far

It isn't hard to see
how Africans in America embraced
a western church.
God was no stranger.
God woke up the day,
      cried over anger,
      calmed the nights with starlight,
          and gave Africans in America serenity as a shield.

We suckled pink babies, didn't kill them.
We turned cheeks, lowered our heads,
but our hearts rose in spirit,
      volcanoes of culture.

I've walked among the hundreds of faces
      humbled in the presence of peace.
I've witnessed the meek,
      the thousand smiles of grace.

Because God called,
Negroes answered as Christian soldiers.
Blacks took to Jesus like
      a crawfish to mud.

God is no stranger in our homes.
We are soldiers at war under Divine charge,
Prayer the only down payment,
        faith the daily deposit.

Whatever the cost of time
God paid in death to Jim Crow, integration,
        Rights, Civil Rights,
        Affirmative selves furnished each generation,
        at least for those about the Lord's business.

The constant cost, a listening heart,
        to the Greatest Voice to echo.
So we rap to the Lord regularly,
        consult on corners at church,
        and in the quiet of a look.
We've come this far by faith.

Afaa Michael Weaver

Thelonius

For Gene F. Thomas

It's as if you are given the sky to carry,
lift it on your shoulders and take it to lunch,
sit in McDonald's with it weighing you down,
this business of being black, of staying black
until the darkness of some eternity kisses you.
Birth gives you something other folk thank
God for not having, or else they pray for it,
to have its gift of a body inclined to touch,
inclined to sing. Yet they will not give back
to God the paleness of being able to touch
absolute power. They envy only for so long,
as being black is being bound to danger.

Among us there are masters like Monk,
who understood the left hand stride
on a brick. In his rapturous dance beside
the piano, he was connected to knowing
the scratch and slide of the shoes leaving
the ground, the shoes of the lynched men.
He carried this thing that we are,
as the mystic he was, revelling in its magic,
respectful of its anger, mute and unchanged
at the hate and envy surrounding us.

One day we learn there is no sky above
this trapped air around the earth.
The sky is but a puff of smoke from
this giant head smoking a Lucky Strike,
pretending not to know the truths.
We learn sometimes in this life,
sometimes in what comes after, where
there is really nothing but everything
we never knew. We learn in silence
the dance Monk knew. We find
secrets for pulling the million arrows
from our souls each time we move

to sleep, to forget that we are both
jewel and jetsam, wanted and unforgiven.

The Poets

1965–1968

In the gymnasium the balls spun
from their fingers like spiders' silk,
fine and unconquerable. Legs woven
in threads of hope, they jumped,
came down on silent sneakers,
dashing any hopes we had of winning.
They were the blacks, the black blacks
who had the advantage of being born.

Dunbar, the high school that sent
a jingle in a broken tongue to colleges
on full scholarships. Dunbar, the high
school that we watched march here
to smash us once again, we black boys
with all these white boys too thick
to dance like a knife in the air,
to open, cut, slice a tangled history.

Breath held back "nigger" in the air
over the bleachers. Breath held back
"wino junkies" under the old clock
over the hollering wooden floor where
we sang pep songs in German, peeping
inside our shirts and ties at our own
magic. The Dunbar Poets made baskets
while strolling, dreaming of rivers.

"Coach, we can't do nothing with
these darkies from Dunbar. Coach,
their bodies ain't bodies. They are
songs from somewhere unfair to us."
We, the black folk at Polytechnic,
wished from the white sea of equality

that Dunbar would stamp blackness
all over this stiff building to save us.

The lead opened so wide it was
too hard for The Poets to keep from
laughing. They slapped their hands
and did the slow jazz of black boys
walking away from an easy game.
In the streets, we watched them stride
away in Florsheims to get high,
too brilliant to live, too brilliant to die.

*R*ita Dove

Freedom Ride

As if, after High Street
and the left turn onto Exchange,
the view would veer onto
someplace fresh: Curacao,
or a mosque adrift on a milk-fed pond.
But there's just more cloud cover,
and germy air
condensing on the tinted glass,
and the little houses with
their fearful patches of yard
rushing into the flames.

Pull the cord a stop too soon, and
you'll find yourself walking
a gauntlet of stares.
Daydream, and you'll wake up
in the stale dark of a cinema,
Dallas playing its mistake over and over
until even that sad reel won't stay
stuck—there's still
Bobby and Malcolm and Memphis,
at every corner the same
scorched brick, darkened windows.

Make no mistake: There's fire
back where you came from, too.
Pick any stop: You can ride
into the afternoon singing with strangers,
or rush home to the scotch
you've been pouring all day—
but where you sit is where you'll be
when the fire hits.

Claudette Colvin Goes to Work

> Another Negro woman has been arrested and thrown into
> jail because she refused to get up out of her seat on the bus
> and give it to a white person. This is the second time since
> the Claudette Colbert [*sic*] case. . . . This must be stopped.
> —Boycott flier, December 5, 1955

Menial twilight sweeps the storefronts along Lexington
as the shadows arrive to take their places
among the scourge of the earth. Here and there
a fickle brilliance—lightbulbs coming on
in each narrow residence, the golden wattage
of bleak interiors announcing *Anyone home?*
or *I'm beat, bring me a beer.*

Mostly I say to myself *Still here.* Lay
my keys on the table, pack the perishables away
before flipping the switch. I like the sugary
look of things in bad light—one drop of sweat
is all it would take to dissolve an armchair pillow
into brocade residue. Sometimes I wait until
it's dark enough for my body to disappear;

then I know it's time to start out for work.
Along the Avenue, the cabs start up, heading
toward midtown; neon stutters into ecstasy
as the make integers light up their smokes and let loose
a stream of brave talk: "Hey Mama" souring quickly to
"Your Mama" when there's no answer—as if
the most injury they can do is insult the reason
you're here at all, walking in your whites
down to the stop so you can make a living.
So ugly, so fat, so dumb, so greasy—
What do we have to do to make God love us?
Mama was a maid; my daddy mowed lawns like a boy,
and I'm the crazy girl off the bus, the one
who wrote in class she was going to be President.

I take the Number 6 bus to the Lex Ave train
and then I'm there all night, adjusting the sheets,
emptying the pans. And I don't curse or spit
or kick and scratch like they say I did then.
I help those who can't help themselves,
I do what needs to be done . . . and I sleep
whenever sleep comes down on me.

Rosa

How she sat there,
the time right inside a place
so wrong it was ready.

That trim name with
its dream of a bench
to rest on. Her sensible coat.

Doing nothing was the doing:
the clean flame of her gaze
carved by a camera flash.

How she stood up
when they bent down to retrieve
her purse. That courtesy.

The Enactment

> I'm just a girl who people were mean to on a bus. . . . I could
> have been anybody.
> —Mary Ware, née Smith

Can't use no teenager, especially
no poor black trash,
no matter what her parents do
to keep up a living. Can't use
anyone without sense enough
to bite their tongue.

It's gotta be a woman,
someone of standing:
preferably shy, preferably married.
And she's got to know
when the moment's right.
Stay polite, though her shoulder's
aching, bus driver
the same one threw her off
twelve years before.

Then all she's got to do is
sit there, quiet, till
the next moment finds her—and only then
can she open her mouth to ask
Why do you push us around?
and his answer: *I don't know but
the law is the law and you
are under arrest.*
She must sit there, and not smile
as they enter to carry her off;
she must know who to call
who will know whom else to call
to bail her out . . . and only then

can she stand up and exhale,
can she walk out the cell
and down the jail steps
into flashbulbs and
her employer's white
arms—and go home,
and sit down in the seat
we have prepared for her.

*O*pal Moore

Eulogy for Sister

Sister married a sometime preacher addicted to silk suits and the chickenfat attentions of christian women who wore unlined pink dresses and hats draped in black netting and were stingy in their smiles mostly reserved for weapons in fierce holy wars, the winners honored to the wretched eternal service of the God/men who seemed always so plentiful yet never sufficient for all the potato salad.

Cancer killed her the certificate said even though for Sister and her preacher/man cancer was no illness but a test of her character meaning she died for lack of faith in the healing hands of her God/man who promised he could petition the Master to save her life if she would but believe in him, and in Him, meaning she died of unbelief, and not of cancer, though she protested her faith shyly into my ear.

She did not want to be healed by doctors when she might conduct a miracle through the hands of her preacher/man, like the five babies she'd birthed she would birth herself a true God/man, a birthing not of her belly yet through the body, spoke to God on it, to be a conduit, to be agency for his uplifting, his coming closer to that higher power. So she prayed cancer into lightning rods, into the power of God, into the cruel hands of a man.

(Maybe she blasphemed to think she would be God's instrument. Maybe her prayers were not humility but a gross boldness. Maybe she failed to predict God's heavenly moodiness.)

She testified to her faith in healing then asked me to sing at her funeral: His Eye is on the Sparrow (and I Know He Watches Me) tipping God off that Sister might not deserve the miracle that awaited only the truly faithful as he tuned in that one day and overheard the sparrow-like chirping whispers she blew into my secret ear though she should have known better—you can't keep a secret from God, and I could not sing her to the grave anyway. It wasn't protocol proper for mourning. I would get frowns.

When I was seventeen I believed Sister could have chosen to keep the life she had. When I was thirty-five I believed she wanted to die.

When I was a woman of a certain age I knew she prayed for a kind of power transforming. The life she had was not enough to live for, but to shame God and save a man's soul, to birth a God out of your own death . . . ? so she reached out, she pulled down a lightning hammer and put it in the hands of the man who took her gifted tool of transforming love and sealed her in her coffin, then turned at her grave side to soak his sweaty grief in the bosom of a woman in unlined black dress and black straw hat draped in pink netting wearing nothing on her face but grateful tears.

oh. sister got bold (didn't she?) died. changed. (didn't she?) changed dying (didn't she, lord. oh, didn't she . . . ?)

The Taste of Life Going On

I have never churned buttermilk. What does it require?
A shaded porch? A natural immunity to tears?
Memories of biscuits and bacon
cold? The way a man holds his neck
as he walks away from hungers
not his own?
A refusal of your eyes to follow him
the way butter runs to the crevices
of warm bread?

Cornelius Eady

How I Got Born

The speaker is the young black man Susan
Smith claimed kidnapped her children

Though it's common belief
That Susan Smith willed me alive
At the moment
Her babies sank into the lake

When called, I come.
My job is to get things done.
I am piecemeal.
I make my living by taking things.

So now a mother needs me clothed
In hand-me-downs
And a knit cap.

Whatever.
We arrive, bereaved
On a stranger's step.
Baby, they weep,
Poor child.

Composite

I am not the hero of this piece.
I am only a stray thought, a solution.
But now my face is stuck to lampposts, glued
To plate glass, my forehead gets stapled
To my hat.

I am here, and here I am not.
I am a door that opens, and out walks
No-one-can-help-you.
Now I gaze, straight into your eye,
From bulletin boards, tree trunks.

I am papered everywhere,
A blizzard called
You see what happens?
I turn up when least expected.
If you decide to buy some milk,

If you decide to wash your car,
If you decide to mail a letter,

I might tumbleweed onto a pant leg.
You can stare, and stare, but I can't be found.
Susan has loosed me on the neighbors,
A cold representative,
The scariest face you could think of.

Birthing

The italicized language is from Susan Smith's
handwritten confession

When I left my home on Tuesday, October 25, I
was very emotionally distraught

I have yet
To breathe.

I am in the back of her mind,
Not even a notion.

A scrap of cloth, the way
A man lopes down a street.

Later, a black woman will say:
"We knew exactly who she was describing."

At this point, I have no language,
No tongue, no mouth.

I am not me, yet.
I am just an understanding.

As I rode and rode and rode, I felt
Even more anxiety.

Susan parks on a bridge,
And stares over the rail.
Below her feet, a dark blanket of river
She wants to pull over herself,
Children and all.

I am not the call of the current.

She is heartbroken.
She gazes down,
And imagines heaven.

*

I felt I couldn't be a good mom anymore, but I didn't want
my children to grow up without a mom.

I am not me, yet.
At the bridge,
One of Susan's kids cries,
So she drives to the lake,
To the boat dock.

I am not yet opportunity.

*

I had never felt so lonely
And so sad.

Who shall be a witness?
Bullfrogs, water fowl.

*

When I was at John D. Long Lake
I had never felt so scared
And unsure.

I've yet to be called.
Who will notice?
Moths, dragonflies,
Field mice.

*

I wanted to end my life so bad
And was in my car ready to
Go down that ramp into
The water

My hand isn't her hand
Panicked on the
Emergency brake.

*

And I did go part way,
But I stopped.

I am not Gravity,
The water lapping against
The gravel.

*

I went again and stopped.
I then got out of the car.

Susan stares at the sinking.
My muscles aren't her muscles,
Burned from pushing.
The lake has no appetite,
But it takes the car slowly,
Swallow by swallow, like a snake.

*

Why was I feeling this way?
Why was everything so bad
In my life?

Susan stares at the taillights
As they slide from here
To hidden.

*

I have no answers
To these questions.

She only has me,
After she removes our hands
From our ears.

Carole B. Weatherford

The Tan Chanteuse

Coquetting through chiffon and rose bouquets,
the tan chanteuse emerged from her Delage,
a panther slinking in a gilded cage,
to sip champagne with counts at chic soirees.
Although she chirped in French at cabarets—
Negresse en deshabille center stage
as primal rhythms fueled her Danse Sauvage—
St. Louis' blues would haunt her all her days.
Banana skirt shirring, a paddle wheel
propelled by her repeated pirouettes,
she turned the blackfaced minstrel of her past
into a new self, so she could forget
the slimy mud where catfish scavenge waste
and lurk amidst debris in stagnant pools.

From Birmingham to Bristol in a Boxcar

Somewhere else, Charles and Furdnor
would have been bronze cowboys
or sepia Gables, sporting pomades,
natty suits with wide, peaked lapels
and squiring svelte chorines
as they stepped from Packards
at premieres. The only bright lights
in Birmingham, though, were furnaces
at foundries; surely hell, they thought.
Their mama had made them choosier
than they could afford, and their daddy
hadn't done them much good neither.
When they buried their mother
and shut up the house, the door closed

on what might have been.
Not inclined to clear trails, dig dams
or blast mountain roads, they nixed
CCC camp, stole away instead, hopping
boxcars the way starlings ride the wind.

Without work or a woman, a man
can either crawl in a hole or decide to never
let grass grow under his feet. Troubles
in gunny sacks, the brothers rode out
the Depression on midnight rattlers, cotton
harvests and close relations in distant towns—
big-hearted aunts with hot meals,
heels of bread and all the advice
they could chew in one sitting.

Queen Ijo's Blues

Willa Mae's battered foot locker holds
a rusty switchblade, the skin a snake shed,
slinky sweat-stained gowns she wore
as Queen Ijo, and snapshots of second-rate acts,
drifters who traveled the carnie circuit
for a season or two then wound up
panhandling for cheap wine.
The bearded lady, she said, cussed
to put a sailor to shame. Every night
when the ferris wheel and cotton candy
ceased spinning, she and Rosetta,
each downed a fifth—bourbon for her.
Rose had helped her choose a tattoo,
a flower now faded, withered
on sagging skin, but still attesting
she was a temptress in her day.

Turban of serpents coiled
around her head, scaly boas dangling
from tawny shoulders and writhing
at her feet, Queen Ijo belted out
broken-heart blues.

Won't let you steal my lovin'
then take me for a ride.
I caught my man two-timin'
and nearly skinned his hide.

Beneath a cloud of tobacco smoke,
a boisterous crowd gathered
on dank summer evenings to ogle freaks.
Siamese twins joined at the thigh,
warmed up for fire-eating contortionists.

By the time Queen took the stage
most spectators were eying plush bears
and snow globes, but heads turned
when she strode out with her entourage,
32 snakes. She was a charmer, yes sirree,
shimmying her hips like no tomorrow,
grime from one-lane highways
rasping in her throat, voice worn
as the motor of an old Chevy pick-up.

Don't need no sugar daddy,
Can't use no pretty boy.
Don't go tryin' to play with me,
'cause I sure ain't no toy.

When she sang of places in the heart, honey,
you better believe she's been there.

Lenard D. Moore

Airport

say that you are a poet
say that you are in New York City
say that you have a suitcase of clothes
a leather bag of toiletries
a briefcase of books, manuscripts, and letters,
say that you leave the suitcase
and the long-strapped leather bag
at the baggage check-in counter
and that your hand cannot release its grip
of the briefcase, brown and swollen.
you walk slowly
send your lies through X-rays
and sit at an island of tables
watching an hour of people come and go
you have just left *CAVE CANEM*
and want someone with you

do you know that someone reels
through the runway of your mind

that someone glides
down the tarmac of your body

that someone waits
in the baggage claim of your heart

do you know

Black Girl Tap Dancing

For Cynthia M. Gary

She taps, pats, clicks,
shoes dazzling the checkered floor,
arms whirl, whirl,
legs cross, uncross,
notes of the feet rise

off tile,
spiral toward the ceiling
of the candlelit Ebony Club.

She pats, clicks, taps
shoes riffing the floor,
arms defy gravity,
legs scissor perfectly,
feet notes soar
from the glossy floor,
scatter from table to table
like fire licking the air.

She clicks, pats, taps
shoes shocking the floor,
arms swirl, whirl,
legs stamp, swing,
feet notes smokebeat
the floor, the floor
just when jazz leaps out of
the hornman's angled trumpet.

She taps, clicks, pats,
this sister firing the floor,
arms propel endless circles,
long legs slide, glide,
displace air, filling space,
red dress snaring the danceway,
black feather bobbing as she taps.

*S*haran Strange

Offering

In the dream, I am burning the rice.
I am cooking for God. I will clean
the house to please Him. So I wash the dishes,
and it begins to burn. It is for luck.
Like rice pelting newlyweds,
raining down, it is another veil,
or an offering that suggests
her first duty: to feed him.

Burning, it turns brown, the color
of my father, whom I never pleased.
Too late, I stand at his bed, calling.
He is swathed in twisted sheets,
a heavy mummy that will not
eat or cry. Will he sleep when
a tall stranger comes to murder me?
Will I die this fourth time, or the next?

When I run it is as if underwater,
slow, sluggish as the swollen grains
rising out of the briny broth to fill the pot,
evicting the steam in low shrieks
like God's breath sucked back in.
Before I slip the black husk of sleep,
I complete the task. The rice chars,
crumbles to dust, to mix with
the salty water, to begin again.

Night Work

In the changeling air before morning
they are silhouettes. Dark ones
with the duskiness of pre-dawn on them
and the shading of dust and sweat.
Busying themselves in buildings,
on scaffolds, and on the black
washed pavements, they are phantoms

of the city—guardians of parking lots,
lobby desks, toll booths, meters,
the all-nights and delivery trucks.
At bus stops they are sentinels
and the drivers. Launderers and cleaners
readying the offices and the untidy houses
of privilege. Cooks heaping up meals
for the well-fed, the disabled or the indifferent.
Trash-takers, making room for more.
Nurses, eternally watching.

When my mother, starting the stove
at 5 am, looked out the window, she saw
her father, days after his funeral.
Had he come back to the field
and the plowing left undone when
the chain snapped and struck him,
knotting his throat into pain
and its aftershock of silence?
Did he return to reclaim the work
like a part of himself unfulfilled
and his story untold?
He is with us still, she said
to the inchoate brightness.
He is there even now.

Spirits are much the same in those
uncensored hours—flitting dim figures,
half-remembered apparitions, whose industry
renews and undergirds our own.
They are our counterparts: the whispering
echo of that other turning
as we turn in bed, the sigh that heaves
in the wake of some unseen act. In the darkness,
where a cycle of making and unmaking unfolds.
If anything could help us believe in
their benign presence, it is the workers,
perpetual as stars, a collective
of eyes and hands, conjuring.

Hunger

1

Combing the papers for summer jobs,
nothing that seems absurd now, or
the obvious hustle, was beneath us;
our need was rampant as newsprint,
those endless columns of pulp dreams.
Not old enough for hire, I fantasized
my fortune in stuffing envelopes.
Seductive ads beckoned: *Make $$$!*
No experience needed! (Just gut-
wrenching desire for anything more . . .)
I'd make thousands, save the family,
buy my way out of loneliness,
invisibility. I sent off letters,
stamps tasting of promise,
expectation swelling in me like a secret.

2

I yearned for glimpses of freedom
like clearings stumbled upon,
meadows of unbroken green
edged by trees, yet seemingly endless.
Like that, but interior, as in the mind's
infinite reaches, hinted at in dreams,
or the openness the heart allows each time
we choose love. Going into fields where
my grandmother eked out a sharecropper's wage,
before I learned they weren't hers,
they too seemed unbounded by horizon.

3

What I wanted I couldn't name,
but the longing felt more real than
what I could touch, constant as labor.
Some nights I lay on the ground for hours,
drunk with that view of the heavens,
as if those thousand thousand stars each
held me by a thread, their imperceptible shuffle

spinning around me some cosmic cocoon.
So I endured the days, and months,
and years that kept me from adulthood,
the time of fulfillment. Or so I thought.
Growing up brought an end
only to a kind of indentured servitude,
taught me to distinguish loss from lack.

4

These days it's TV commercials—
the happy clan hawking cars and
fortified cereals—a kind of contentment
bartered for with longing or need.
Anything is attainable in fantasy.
It takes so much to learn just this:
The things we need we don't get in this world.
Some say we're lucky to be alive, to have
our chance each day, to fight, get by. I say
what's luck, or chance, or choice for that matter?
I take the offerings of this slim life,
hunger, like memory, some kind of assurance,
the body, open, unable to be filled.

Adisa Vera Beatty

Distance

What exists of you I have spread thin and think of when
I will not be able to borrow or secret away anymore of your
belongings, your dress socks already eliminating themselves,
taking up silence, leaving space, allowing you to become shadowy

Remembered details are now punches, surprises, unestimated
something I had no reason to protect myself from, pictures
of you smiling, that small gap between your two front teeth

That same gap in my teeth, but later out grew, the teeth
      straightened
themselves, then years later as if they too carried memory,
      huddled,
pushed together, to forget what was gone

Like the mornings of that first year when I would catalog and
      recount
each disappearance, a hair brush, shaving kit, shoes, the closet of
      suits,
dusty outlines of pictures removed, leaving this opening

Memorization

I know how it happened and it has been a long time
but those details I was ushered away from have come back

and if I am ever in pain, seeing my brother in a winter coat,
baseball cap and book bag, carefully locking the front door,
my mother pushing on the backs of earrings, or me looking
to see if you have finally taken over my face

you were alone, your mind, body vulnerable
the bald spot on your head where I have placed my hand,
felt blood chugging back and forth in silent communication

the smooth hands with short nails and half moons,
one raised in a blur a bullet went through, two, a bullet

in the chest and glistening ruby red blood jumped out, three,
a bullet in the neck, and still wanting to breathe, you choked
and spit red—a language

Geography

This is a hurtful thing, when your memory fails you,
buckling under times weight, even worse for those
that shunned pictures, had no video camera

And if the dead have memory you too perhaps are remembering
in patches, like family quilts, disintegrating nods to Ancestors

Memories were so vivid, I'd flinch at the smells; cologne,
leather wingtips, hygiene, blood warmed skin

Now there's me feeble minded, blind, stumbling, what if you have
taken the form of something or someone else coming back to me,
I may not even have the sense to know

And you may not recognize your child, seven years later, shadows
have touched my face, you would hate the uncombed hair, it's
    resilience,
it's desire for growth, the inked tattoos, I have stopped piercing
    my ears

I am leaving for you hieroglyphs, markings in the road,
    watermarks
on my surface, scratches, the faded burn on my arm, ear marks
    for you,
so that I may be recognized

Elizabeth Alexander

The Josephine Baker Museum

1. East St. Louis (1918)
Mama danced
a glass
of water balanced
on her head.

"Someone raped
a white woman!
We ran
at night,
next day
heard tell

of eyes
plucked out,
of scalps
pulled clean,
a bloody sky.

That day
God showed
his face,
grey and shaggy,
in the rain clouds.

2. Costumes
The black and white checked overalls
I wore off the boat at Le Havre. Wired skirts
whose trains weigh fifty pounds. Furling,
curling headpieces, and hourglass-
shaped gowns.

Schiparellis and Poirets! The green suede
Pilgrim shoes and orange jacket,
Harlem-made. The lime chiffon!
the one with egrets
painted on.

I'm sick of *touts le bananes*. Ici,
my uniform: French Air Force, fray-spots

blackened back with ink. And here,
the diamond necklace,
for my glorious Chiquita.

3. The Wig Room
A gleaming black sputnik of hair.
A solid figure-eight of hair, glazed black.
Crows' wings of hair, a waist-length switch.

Black profiteroles of mounded hair.
Hair like a Eiffel Tower, painted black.
A ziggurat of patent leather hair.

Black crowns to be taken on and off, that live
in the room when the lights go out, a roomful
of whispering Josephines, a roomful
of wigs in the dark.

4. Ablutions
In the cinema Mammy hands Scarlett
white underthings to cover her white skin.
I am both of them and neither, tall,
tan, terrific, soaking in my tub of milk.

What would it mean to be me on stage
in a bathtub soaping, singing my French
chansons with one pointed foot with painted toes
suggesting what is underneath, suggesting

dusky, houri dreams and is she really
naked? Do they really want to see
the nappy pussy underneath that sweats
and stinks and grinds beneath bananas,

turns to seaweed in the tub? What if
I let my hair go back, or dressed
more often as a man? What if I let myself
get fat? What would it mean to step out

of the bathtub onto the stage and touch
myself, do to myself what I do to myself

in the bedroom when only my animals
watch? What would I be to my audience then?

(Sigh) Come here, baby. Dry me off.

5. Diva Studies
What is original, what
is facsimile? The boys
in the dressing room are showing
me how to skin my hair down flat
like patent leather, black as that.
I show them how to paint eyeballs
on their eyelids to look bright
from the last row, how I line
my eyes like the Egyptian cat.
We carry on, in that dingy,
musky, dusty room overhung
with fraying costumes, peeling
sequins, shedding feathers, mules
with broken heels, mending glue, eye-
lash glue, charcoal sticks and matches,
brushes and unguents and bottles of oil.
The dressing room is my schoolhouse.
My teachers are men more woman
than actual women, and I
am the skinny sixteen-year old
whose hair is slicked flat because
Congoleum burned it off.
I cross my eyes and knock my knees,
am somehow still a diva.
The boys swoop past and are rare.
The beauty is how this strange
trade works. The truth of it is,
we are fabulous.

At the Beach

Looking at the photograph is somehow not
unbearable: My friends, two dead, one low

on T-cells, his white T-shirt an X-ray
screen for the virus, which I imagine
as a single, swimming paisley, a sardine
with serrated fins and a neon spine.

I'm on a train, thinking about my friends
and watching two women talk in sign language.
I feel the energy and heft their talk
generates, the weight of their words in the air
the same heft as your presence in this picture,
boys, the volume of late summer air at the beach.

Did you tea-dance that day? Write poems
in the sunlight? Vamp with strangers? There is
sun under your skin like the gold Sula
found beneath Ajax's black. I calibrate
the weight of your beautiful bones, the weight
of your elbow, Melvin,
                              on Darrell's brown shoulder.

Passage

Henry Porter wore good clothes for his journey,
the best his wife could make from leftover
cambric, shoes stolen from the master. They
bit his feet, but if he took them off he feared
he'd never get them on again. He needed
to look like a free man when he got there.
Still in a box in the jostling heat,
nostrils to a board pried into a vent,
(a peephole, too, he'd hoped, but there was only
black to see) there was nothing to do
but sleep and dream and weep. Sometimes the dreams
were frantic, frantic loneliness an acid
at his heart. Freedom was near but un-
imaginable. Anxiety roiled inside
of him, a brew which corroded his stomach,
whose fumes clamped his lungs and his throat.
When the salt-pork and cornbread were finished

he dreamed of cream and eggs but the dreams
made him sick. He soiled himself and each time
was ashamed. He invented games, tried to
remember everything his mother
ever told him, every word he hadn't
understood, every vegetable he'd ever
eaten (which was easy: kale, okra, corn,
carrots, beans, chard, yams, dandelion greens),
remember everyone's name who had ever
been taken away. The journey went that way.
When he got there, his suit was chalky
with his salt, and soiled, the shoes waxy with blood.
The air smelled of a surfeit of mackerel.
Too tired to weep, too tired to look through
the peephole and see what freedom looked like,
he waited for the man to whom he'd shipped
himself: Mister William Still, Undertaker,
Philadelphia. He repeated the last
words he'd spoken to anyone: goodbye
wife Clothilde, daughter Eliza,
best friend Luke. Goodbye, everyone, goodbye.
When I can, I'll come for you. I swear,
I'll come for you.

Jabari Asim

1st Lt. Vernon J. Baker: Hero on the Hill

(Company C, 370th Infantry Regiment, 92nd Division)

We go up twenty-five strong.
I'm fresh from OCS,
lectures, lessons
ringing in my head.
Press on.
Set an example.
Complete the mission.

Textbooks and games fade fast
when the real thing hits.
We're headed up Hill X in Italy.
Castle Aghinolfi is close enough
to spit at.
How many Nazis are between us
and its ancient stones,
scowling at the dark mystery
gathering below?

We charge
and the air around us changes,
grows heavy with horror
and gray shapes shuffling,
dim outlines of dugouts
and telescopes.
Forward through fear, fury
and the nerve-scraping screech
of artillery, we climb.
We keep our eyes
on the castle, our M-1's aimed
at the hatred ahead.

The ground gives way
to Nazis in our hair
wide-eyed and howling,
eager to take us out
all at once or one by one.

I take seven Germans by myself,
kicking in their teeth
with my rifle and my rage.
All around me my own men fall,
slashed and screaming,
their hearts bursting into
bloody chunks.

At OCS our chief of staff said,
"Now it's time for the colored boys
to go get killed."
My company commander,
his pale face flickering red,
runs for reinforcements.
I never see him again.

Killing works two ways.
We blink back blood
and fight until a strange stillness
swallows us up.
Twenty-six Germans
lie twisted beneath our boots.
Their machine gun nests,
their lookout posts and dugouts,
all smoke and splinters now.

Seven of us survive,
sliding and stumbling
until the bottom of the hill
swells to meet our feet.
I sense my stomach
turning against me,

bones and ash under my eyelids,
the smell of flesh
ripped and rotting in the dark.

Let's Just Tell It

For Henry Dumas

Take my soul up and plant it again.
–H.D., *Ark of Bones*

1
laugh
talk
joke

mess with me
if you must
face a flaming arrow
flung from a cloud of dust

2
Sweet Home, Arkansas:
redolent of rednecks
rich in razorbacks
and rural rhythms

where the long cloak of cotton
lingers in fingers
where the river rolls
and the damp clay clings
to a black bard's rememberings:

the ox and the bow
the rock church and the shack row
the fox and the crow

3
Gospel grew in him,
dark throats hailing heaven
silver swans sweet and surreal,
all eloquence and ecstasy.
Choirs on fire with swamp-fever fervor.
God taking root in homespun harmonies.

4
Next stop, New York.
A ten-year-old's toughest test,
this tempestuous town.

From fatback to fast blacks,
sons of Msippi
turned Harlem hustlers.
Hip-tongued talkers in two-tone shoes
electrifying the Delta blues.

5
A dizzying decade.
The poet comes of age.
Brownstones form a concrete cage.

The Air Force teases:
A poet can see the world
and do as he pleases.
Besides, the vision needs
to taste fruit grown from foreign seeds.

Ride a rope of wind.
Oceans, provinces, peninsulas unfold.

got to get home and spread the news
got the Uncle Sam Uptight Blues
got to get home and spread the news
got the Uncle Sam Uptight Blues

6
He'd known the heat
of Arabian sand,
simooms singeing a settlement square,
uprooting man, camel, muezzin
and leaving nothing, not even air.
No heat, though, like that of love.

Loretta is a tiger fish,
slashing the shores of his blood.
Their union is a song of flesh.

i am thy mate and thy strength and thy song
aiwa aiwa

The god-sound trembles in her belly.
Sons rise from a circle of dust.

7
Another decade,
this one deadly.
Marked by martyrdom.
In the background,
flaming streets.
Rage flows.

Dumas is ready.
A galloping griot,
gap-toothed and goateed
razor-thin and righteous.
An upward bounder
through tenements and tent cities,
taking aim at Southern sickness.

His life burns brightly:
Husband
Father
World Watcher
Dream Channeler

His genius blossoms
in bluesman moans,
a prophet boy conjuring bones.
His truth forms a long song born
in the bell of an afro-horn,

blown softly
under the eye of the moon
into the bloody face of the river
beneath the shadow of shuddering leaves
astride the drumbeat of deathless spirits
above the rumbling of the falling rock
beyond the cry of the kingless crowd

over the wails of the feverish desert
within the guts and scales of dead fish
by a poet shrinking in a halo of blood

8
Dead at 34.

Nothing unique in this exit:
A badge.
A bullet.
A black man bleeding.

Swift.
Sour.
Abrupt.

Curious.
Cruel.
Corrupt.

Blood runs like ink,
redolent of rails
and subway stink.

9
Aba
Aba
Consecrate these bones.

Aba
Aba
Prophesy this name.

Dumas
Dumas

Play a blood-crashing chord
in memory of his genius,

a brilliant blooming
a resilient funk

a luminous lyric
for the songless
and the dead.

Baby's Breath

For Nia, at 2 weeks

Daughter, while you rest
I monitor the movement
Of your sleeping breast,

Watch it dip and swell:
Undulant, radiating
Newborn baby smell.

Precious air floats through
Your delicate, thirsty throat,
Helps me to eschew

Stirrings of distrust:
Can your lungs protect you from
Cruelties of dust?

They're too new, I think,
This fresh but fragile pair, too
Innocent and pink

To endure a sneeze
Or other harbingers of
Pollen and disease.

Remember, honey,
Inhale. Exhale. In. Out. Ahh.
Isn't it funny

How a single breath
Contains lifetimes? Consider:
God. Love. Hunger. Death.

Whole philosophies
May merge and divide in a
Solitary breeze,

A gust of wordplay
Whirling among friends on an
Ordinary day.

Make worlds, little girl,
Breathe galaxies and stars. While
I caress a curl

Of luminous hair,
A ringlet dancing in the
Ecstasy of air.

Joel Dias-Porter

(DJ Renegade)

Fireflies in a Jar

My best friend Bruce
is allergic to bees.
One time he got stung
and swelled up
like a vacuum cleaner bag.
His mother had to give him a shot,
he couldn't come out for two days.
The Encyclopedia say
if bees sting you, they die.
Bruce say grasshoppers
spit tobacco juice,
sometimes we catch'em
and pull they legs off.
The legs keep on jumping.
Every time it rains,
worms be making the letter "S"
on the sidewalk.
If you step on one,
your shoes get real slippery.
Encyclopedia say they
male and female in one body.
Yesterday I saw a silverfish
in my toy box,
it had a million legs
and bent like a bracelet.
If one bites you
your fingernails'll fall off.
I saw a pregnant roach too,
I'm the best roach killer
in our building.
Encyclopedia say roaches carry disease,
but I ain't never seen a sick roach.
Bruce say you can tell a project roach,
cuz they don't run
when you cut on the lights.
At night I sneak in the kitchen
to see what roaches be doing
when nobody's around,

Encyclopedia say in some countries
people eat insects,
I wonder if they eat roaches?
Sometimes me and Bruce
go down to the laundry room
and squash waterbugs.
If you real quiet,
you can hear
the shells scrunch.
Spiders around here
are little and yellow,
except Daddy Long-Legs.
Encyclopedia say they ain't spiders
but LaTricia still screams
if you put one on her.
Bruce say he saw two Black Widows
in the laundry room
hissing like cats.
I don't believe him,
his mother wouldn't let him
in the laundry room by hisself.
When it's night enough,
God turns on the fireflies.
Last week we caught some
in a Coke bottle.
Bruce gave them
to this girl Terri he likes,
she washed'em out
and got a nickel for the bottle.
I told him he shoulda
gave her a caterpillar,
Encyclopedia say they turn into butterflies
and all girls like butterflies.
Bruce say there's Nature
in the woods behind our projects.
But everybody knows
Nature's in Encyclopedias.
Them bee stings must
do something to his brain
cuz Bruce be tripping.

Thursday Poem

I'm laying across a leather couch with Maria,
her half-Mexican mouth and *chile* green eyes
watch Jordan float all over the court.
It's been six days since I've seen you,
now my head sinks into the soft of her thigh
as Jordan wins the game with a long jumper.
We cheer, then kill the TV and chill.
In the speakers on her mantle, it's *Round Midnight*
but she doesn't want my hands stroking her leg
and her fingers refuse to enter my hair
as though frightened by my need to be touched.
I don't know how to ask her to hold me,
so I make excuses and roll from her crib.
It's too late for the subway, so I walk,
the air swipes its sweaty hands across my face
and thirteen blocks from First St. NW,
I pass where Charlie's Seafood used to be
and remember that day I had only two dollars,
but bought some sweet potato pie for $1.50,
then came up to your apartment without calling.
Your eyeball asks *Who is it?* through the peephole,
I yell *Me, and a slice of your favorite pie.*
You crack the door, eye me like an errant child,
your lips red as pistachio shells.
Don't ever do this again you say, then let me in.
You make apple cinnamon tea, say *Let's play dominoes.*
We turn a box over and plop on big pillows,
you shuffle the bones and count out seven,
turning yours on their sides so I can't see.
I gather mine around me like tiny tombstones.
After whupping me twice and talking much trash,
you lay on your back with your numbers facing up,
your mouth blank beneath the black dots of your eyes.
I align your spine like a row of dominoes
then feed you sweet potato pie from a plastic fork
that almost melts as it touches your lips.
I consider letting you have the whole crust
but you say *Let's split it, like a wishbone.*

I scoot close, brush hair from your shoulder
as you lean into the rhythm of my hand.
Your fingers tip-toe up the back of my neck
and a smile curls your cherry licorice lips.
Now, I'm at the corner of Seventh and Florida Ave.,
wondering if this red light will ever change.
And no matter how much I try to deny it,
the thought of your fingertips tingles my ear
and it's clear I don't just want you. I need you.
Not like the letter Q needs to be followed by U,
but like a small i needs the pupil that dots it.

Subterranean Night-Colored Magus

3 Moods in the Mode of Miles

Subterranean means underground
       deep, profound
wasn't Miles one deep brother
       deep as a mine shaft
       decrescendoing to the motherlode
       blue blowing undersongs
Miles on tenor trumpet
       ten or eleven levels deeper
       than the next cat
       painting all up under the canvas
       making it bleed All Blues
       out the other side
Blowing subterranean solos
       underground rhythmic resistance
       visual virtuoso
       battling musical mafiosos
       burrowing under they skin
Miles, son of a dentist doing rootwork
       with a hoodoo horn hollering Bebop toasts
He Petey Wheatstraw
       Satchmo's son-in-law
       a Signifyin Junkie jumping cold turkey
       out the Lion's mouth

Shine below the deck of the Titanic
blueing up the boilers
Miles could blue like Bird
freight like Trane
early like Bird
night like Trane
wing like Bird
rail like Trane
Rumbling underground.

Nightcolor is blacker
than a million miles of fresh asphalt
wasn't Miles a deepblack brother
black and fluid as floating smoke
black as the sky round midnight
black as a tire turning for miles ahead
black kettle stewing a Bitch's Brew
so black, he was Kind of Blue
Miles, slick as black ice
cool as black snow
sweet as black cherries
On the Downbeat like a blackjack
a black jackhammer
black Jack Johnson
black jack of all trumpeting trades
Miles, Jack of Spades
was our Ace cuz he played
nightcolors
Deepblack, tripleblack
shinyblack,
cinderblack
ashyblack,
quarterblack
multi-meta-megablack
All shades of Miles
shifting harmonic gears
in his chromatic Ferrari
Blowing Blue Moods
with his black turned

to the audience
speaking cooly
in the colors of night.

Magi are priests
spell-wailing wizards
wasn't Miles a deepblackmagic brother
Magus, Magus? ask minders
of the metronome
Miles is secular they say
but we know you spiritual
a soloing sorcerer with E.S.P.
Lord have mercy
you Rev. Miles tonally testifyin
from the Book of the Blues
blowing muted magic
as chapter and verse
Making a joyful noise
unto the Lord
or anybody hip enough
to dig the scene
You Magi Miles with crazy styles
even sported a Tutu
Miles, 1.6 sacred klicks of cool
5,280 feet doing
the East Saint Boogie
moody as any Monk
you were Live and Evil
but In a Silent Way
Your holy brown hands
cast brass ornamentation
cast a net of chorded notes
cast Milestones through
the stained-glass windows of Jazz
conjuring in the key of We
so deeply, so darkly, such magic.

Thomas Sayers Ellis

Sir Nose D'VoidofFunk

1

That name: D'VoidofFunk.
An expressionistic thing

With do-loops
And threes in it,

Preceded by
A silly-serious

Attempt by
Old Smell-O-Vision

To cop
Some nobility.

2

The whole bumpnoxious,
Dark thang stanks
Of jivation

And Electric Spank.
Glory, glory, glory-
hallastoopid.

Then there's his funny
Accent–pitch
Change and delay

Looped through
Feedback, pre-spankic
Self-satisfunktion.

Nose gets harder
As his voice
Gets higher.

Nose won't take
His shoes off,
Dance, swim or sweat.

Nose snores,
A deep snooze,
Snoozation.

3

Syndrome tweedle dee dum. Despite
The finger-pointing profile,
False peace signs
And allergic reaction

To light, we brothers
Wanna be down
With Nose. All that!
The girls, the clothes.

Now you know Nose
Knows when to fake it
And when to fake
Faking it.

            Waves
Don't mean he's gone
Or that there's going
To be a cover-up,
Very Nixonian.

You can't impeach Nose.
Where's your court-
room, your wig and robe?
You ain't Nose judge.

Somebody scream just to see
The look on our party's
Tromboneless face,
That burial ground

Of samples and clones
Jes grew. A nose
Is a nose is a nose
Is a nose,

so
Wherever the elephants
In his family
Tree untrunk
Is home.

4

And that's about the only tail
Mugs can push or pin
On him.

View of the Library of Congress
from Paul Laurence Dunbar High School

For Doris Craig and Michael Olshausen

A white substitute teacher
At an all-Black public high school,
He sought me out saying my poems
Showed promise, range, a gift,
And had I ever heard of T. S. Eliot?
No. Then Robert Hayden perhaps?

Hayden, a former colleague,
Had recently died, and the obituary
He handed me had already begun
Its journey home—from the printed page
Back to tree, gray becoming
Yellow, flower, dirt.

No river, we skipped rocks
On the horizon, above Ground Zero,
From the roof of the Gibson Plaza Apartments.
We'd aim, then shout the names
Of the museums, famous monuments,
And government buildings

Where our grandparents, parents,
Aunts, and uncles worked. Dangerous duds.

The bombs we dropped always fell short,
Missing their mark. No one, not even
Carlton Green who had lived in
As many neighborhoods as me,

Knew in which direction
To launch when I lifted Hayden's
Place of employment–
The Library of Congress–
From the obituary, now folded
In my back pocket, a creased map.

We went home, asked our mothers
But they didn't know. Richard's came
Close: Somewhere near Congress,
On Capitol Hill, take the 30 bus,
Get off before it reaches Anacostia,
Don't cross the bridge into Southeast.

The next day in school
I looked it up–the National Library
Of the United States in Washington, D.C.
Founded in 1800, open to all taxpayers
And citizens. *Snap!* My Aunt Doris
Works there, has for years.

Once, on her day off, she
Took me shopping and bought
The dress shoes of my choice.
Loafers. They were dark red,
Almost purple, bruised–the color
Of blood before oxygen reaches it.

I was beginning to think
Like a poet, so in my mind
Hayden's dying and my loafers
Were connected, but years apart,
As was Dunbar to other institutions–
Ones I could see, ones I could not.

John Keene

After C (3): Tayloriana

I have to find it again, an extreme music. Inspired by voicings: out, but I may lose it again. That I may live it, utterly beautiful in its rendering. The brink of composition, brink of the hand called looking. And open, drawing like flying open alone, broken without having to take me. Musically it was composition of a distant whiteness, where absence too was thrown, by concentration alone, but not in the listening. Drawing. A profound transitional, kaleidoscopic, where the axes of decay were really the depiction. Dark seisms really come to mind, the first death and the last one, each darker, these first, these powerful, arranged as a collection. Arranged, not solo. At that time I was collecting other pieces, hands, the electronic composed as an album. Looking as some other thing. But I may pick another break, piece the track. In concert. I've since thrown it. He called the depth extraordinary. A fearful copy.

The Haymarket

no longer slings back rot-gut G&Ts before 2 a.m.,
as the doors close. These days, like the Napolean,
Sporters, Bohemian, the Zone itself, it's a monument
to pure memory, but it already was dying
the evening we went to hear Jennifer Holiday
wail "And I'm Telling You," and jointly remarked how far
she'd fallen since the Kilimanjaro of Dreamgirls. Re-connecting
with her audience base is another way of putting it,
and she missed not a single note, hunched over that microphone,
song after song sweating through her spangles
like a dockworker, as men slid to and fro in shade
in front of the box stage. That was the night you tore
out my throat over my words with an ex, who you'd hurled
from your car years before when you first encountered
his tales of woe, whom later I observed sneak
out of Keller's to avoid a Brooklyn ass-whupping.
I wanted to remember that as the night two drag queens
tall as Masai threw down in front of the Dumpsters,
hurling pumps and wigs like gladiators, and a carnival-
sized crowd swelled the lot, pacing the glass, chatting,

cruising, watching the battle, as Warren offered play-by-play
(knowing the full tea) and Johnny offered up beauty
in a snaggled grin and slender Darrell, laughing, a cap
over his velvety brow, re-introduced himself to me,
who hadn't yet moved into love's house with you. But
that mêlée too occurred summers before, when that club
still felt new as a gift, alive, dangerous—though not as bad
as they'd warned us—and every man met I recalled
by name and face, half-believing I'd never see them again
because they'd disappear into wrong numbers conceived
on the spot, or ragged married lives, or the shadows
that only grew rattier in the club's corners when you drank
too much, or danced too much, or learned that someone else
you liked and hoped to hook up with had passed and you
stepped outside without a ride and missed the T knowing no taxis
were going to ferry you all the way back to Western Avenue
for less than $10, in that indifferent midnight Boston rain.

Natasha Trethewey

Limen

All day I've listened to the industry
of a single woodpecker, worrying the catalpa tree
just outside my window. Hard at his task,

his body is a hinge, a door knocker
to the cluttered house of memory in which
I can almost see my mother's face.

She is there, again, beyond the tree,
its slender pods and heart-shaped leaves,
hanging wet sheets on the line—each one

a thin white screen between us. So insistent
is this woodpecker, I'm sure he must be
looking for something else—not simply

the beetles and grubs inside, but some other gift
the tree might hold. All day he's been at work,
tireless, making the green hearts flutter.

Bellocq's Ophelia

—From a photograph, circa 1912

In Millais' painting, Ophelia dies face up,
eyes and mouth open as if caught in the gasp
of her last word or breath, flowers and reeds
growing out of the pond, floating on the surface
around her. The young woman who posed
lay in a bath for hours, shivering,
catching cold—perhaps imagining fish
tangling in her hair or nibbling a dark mole
raised upon her white skin. Ophelia's final gaze
aims skyward, her palms curling open
as if she's just said *take me.*

I think of her when I see Bellocq's photograph—
a woman posed on a wicker divan, her hair

spilling over. Around her, flowers—
on a pillow, on a thick carpet. Even
the ravages of this old photograph
bloom like water lilies across her thigh.
How long did she hold there, this other
Ophelia, nameless inmate of Storyville,
naked, her nipples offered up hard with cold?

The small mound of her belly, the pale hair
of her pubis—these things—her body
there for the taking. But in her face, a dare.
Staring into the camera, she seems to pull
all movement from her slender limbs
and hold it in her heavy-lidded eyes.
Her body limp as dead Ophelia's,
her lips poised to open, to speak.

Drapery Factory, Gulfport, Mississippi, 1956

She made the trip daily, though
later she would not remember
how far to tell the grandchildren—
better that way.
She could keep those miles
a secret, and her black face
and black hands, and the pink bottoms
of her black feet
a minor inconvenience.

She does remember the men
she worked for, and that often
she sat side by side
with white women, all of them
bent over, pushing into the hum
of the machines, their right calves
tensed against the pedals.

Her lips tighten speaking
of quitting time when

the colored women filed out slowly
to have their purses checked,
the insides laid open and exposed
by the boss's hand.

          But then she laughs
when she recalls the soiled Kotex
she saved, stuffed into a bag
in her purse, and Adam's look
on one white man's face, his hand
deep in knowledge.

Major Jackson

Indian Song

Freddie Hubbard's playing the cassette deck
Forty miles outside Hays and I've looked at
This Kansas sunset for three hours now, sipping
Gin-and-tonics, almost bristling as big rigs bounce
And grumble along I-70. At this speed cornfields come
In splotches, murky yellows and greens abutting
The road's shoulder, the flat wealth of the nation whirring by.
It's a kind of ornamentation I've gotten used to–
As in a dream. Espaliered against the sky's blazing–
Cloud-luffs cascade lace-like darkening whole fields.
30,000 feet above someone is buttering a muffin.
Someone stares at a skyphone, and momentarily–
A baby's cry in pressurized air. Through double-paned squares
Someone squints: fields cross-hatched by asphalt-strips.
Light over earth is a patchwork of goodbyes.
It is said Cézanne looked at a landscape so long he felt
As if his eyes were bleeding. No matter that. I'm heading west–
It's all too redolent, the wailing music, the fields of sunflowers,
You by my side subtracting miles traveled from miles to go.

Block Party

For The Roots

Woofers stacked to pillars made a disco of a city-block.
Turn these rhymes down a notch and you can hear
the child in me reverb on that sidewalk where
a microphone mushroomed with a Caliban's cipher.
Those couplets could rock a party from here to Jamaica;
its code was simple . . . *Prospero's a sucker emcee.*
Smoke rising off a grill threatens to cloud this memory;
my only light, the urinous cones of streetlamps.
Did not that summer crowd bounce in ceremonial fits?
Ah yes! It was the DJ and his spinning TECHNICS delicately
needling a groove, something from James Brown,
FUNKY PRESIDENT; then, working the cross-fade
like a lightswitch, he composed a stream of scratches,
riffs. Song broken down to a dream of song flows

from my pen; the measured freedom coming off this page
was his pillared spell of drums . . . it kept the peace;
a police-car idled indifferently at the other end
of the street. What amount of love can express
enough gratitude for those reformulations, life ruptured,
then looped back, def and gaudy like those *phat,*
gold chains? Keep to sampling language; keep it
boomin' like Caliban yelling, *Somebody! Anybody! Scream!*

To Afaa Michael S. Weaver

Bless your writer's hand, Sir, and its paternal blues.
Tonight Kala grazes a palm over a battered face,
feeling his newborn features in a Correction's zoo
the shock is permanent like the caged primate
who suddenly detects he's human. A Homo Erectus
stands upright on guard outside his cell.
For the record, good friend, tropes are brutal,
relentless, miraculous as a son's birth. KING KONG'S
memoir gets repeated on the evening news
like a horror flick and everywhere dark men
are savagely ambushed. So, when a woman strolls
towards a homeless BIGGER, the audience
tenses up involuntarily beneath a cone of light.
This is the work of blockbusters: Kala's groan
twisting a steel cot, and by morning's sunlight,
your cramped hand. Pages pile to a tome
on a kitchen table, and its defense is three-fifths
human, two-fifths man. I await its world premiere;
til then, when the soul hears of black guards who strike
harder, the brain goes arthritic, tropes proliferate,
and a wide-screen blooms with images of heavyweights
whose gloved hands struggle to balance a pen.

Some Kind of Crazy

It doesn't matter if you can't see
Steve's 1985 CORVETTE: turquoise-colored,

Plush purple seats, gold-trimmed
Rims that make little stars in your eyes

As if the sun is kneeling
At the edge of sanity. Like a Baptist
Preacher stroking the dark underside
Of God's wet tongue, he can make you

Believe. It's there, his scuffed wing-
Tips, ragged as a mop, shuffling
Concrete, could be ten-inch FIRESTONE
Wheels, his vocal chords fake

An eight cylinder engine that wags
Like a dog's tail as he shifts gears. Imagine
Steve moonstruck, cool, turning right
Onto RIDGE AVENUE, arms forming

Arcs, his hands a set of stiff *C's*
Overthrowing each other's rule,
His lithe body and head snap back
Pushing a stick-shift into fourth

Whizzing past UNCLE SAM'S PAWN
SHOP, past CHUNG PHAT'S STOP & GO.
Only he knows his destination,
His limits. Can you see him? Imagine

Steve, moonstruck, cool, parallel
Parking between a PAGER and a PINTO–
Obviously the most hip backing up,
Head over right shoulder, one hand

Spinning as if polishing a dream;
And there's Tina, wanting to know
What makes a man tick, wanting
A one-way trip to the stars.

We, the faithful, never call
Him crazy, crack-brained, just a little
Touched. It's all he ever wants:
A car, a girl, a community of believers.

Kevin Young

Quivira City Limits

For Thomas Fox Averill

Pull over. Your car with its slow
breathing. Somewhere outside Topeka

it suddenly all matters again,
those tractors blooming rust

in the fields only need a good coat
of paint. Red. You had to see

for yourself, didn't you; see that the world
never turned small, transportation

just got better; to learn
we can't say a town or a baseball

team without breathing in
a dead Indian. To discover why Coronado

pushed up here, following the guide
who said he knew fields of gold,

north, who led them past these plains,
past buffaloes dark as he was. Look.

Nothing but the wheat, waving them
sick, a sea. While they strangle

him blue as the sky above you
The Moor must also wonder

when will all this ever be enough?
this wide open they call discovery,

disappointment, this place my
thousand bones carry, now call home.

Everywhere Is out of Town

For Maceo Parker & the JB Horns

Beanville. Tea
party. Five black cats
& a white boy. Chitlin
circuit. Gravy colored suits,
preacher stripes. Didn't
know you could buy
muttonchops these days.
Afros. Horns slung
round necks like giant
ladles. Dressing. Uptempo
blessing: *Good God*

everywhere! We bow our
heads before the band
lets loose. Drummer unknown
as a hymn's third verse.
Older woman pushes toward
the front, catching the spirit
like the crazy lady at church
six scotches later, Communion
breath. Hands waving. Sweaty
face rags, post-sermon
mop, suicidal white girls crying
like the newly baptized. All that
water. Play it. Swing
it. *Be suggestive.* Request
"Chicken" & "Pass the Peas"
like we used to say. Have mercy!
Thanksgiving's back in town

& we're all crammed in the club white
as the walls of a church basement. Feet
impatient as forks. Only ten bucks
a plate for this leftover band. Thigh,
drumsticks, neck. Dark meat.

East Jesus

The South knows ruin & likes it
thataway–the barns becoming
earth again, leaning in–
SAW CHAIN on a sign somewhere
between Boonies & Sticks, pop.
10, now 9, now 11 (the Bloodworth
twins). Here, in East Jesus

the water tower is about half-
empty, the only bar (next county
over) LA TAVERN & TACKLE SHOP
stays full. THE FUTURE
PLANT FOR IT NOW some signs
might say, but we like our trees
fallen, or cut, or bent precarious

above our houses, about to become
fire. Termites & tow trucks & the Sheriff
Dept in which we each are deputies, except
those who ain't, who never will be. The no
good know it, and love that too–
our newspaper's police blotter bulges

with last night's stars, arrests,
their drunken fingers smudged
into night. Sleep it off
& tomorrow's another yesterday–AVOID
SINS TRAGEDY   LEARN SATANS
STRATEGY our roadside church
announces whiles we sit & pray & can't

hardly wait to make love or have
that drink, hungering through
the sermon & shouts–stomachs bunched
as if underwear. Benediction–
handshakes smelling of chicken
served after church–before crossing
the worn-down (ain't this where Sis
was struck dead) tracks, tall with weeds–

POETIC RETROSPECTIVE

Garrett McDowell

A Blooming in the Valley

For Joanne Gabbin

> The time
> cracks into furious flower. . . .
> And sways in wicked grace.
> –Gwendolyn Brooks

1

We heard the rumbling drum song.
She had already beckoned Shu to send the winds,
let libations wet the face of sunrise,
spanned the mountains with her chanting
over rivers, into urban canyons,
reaching the ears of mediums.

We had talked about her medicine,
her vision, wide like the view
from a corner apartment higher up,
seeing both ways; about
her gait, producing
motion in her wake–

boulders turned aside
where the poets arrive, here,
amazed at a clearing placed
in the purified valley air.
Here, to define and medicate.
Our mediums to deities who,

before they swam the riptide, lit the sun,
before they crossed the Mississippi, sailed the Nile.

2

They came drawn by the furious muse.
Staccato singing tells us
Shu has welcomed them,
sirocco breezes whirling the hall
like bellowing southeasterly seas,
an unexpected rush
through the Shenandoah,
jolting with the pulse of centuries.

We know him
in the twist and strut of the trees
like seasoned weathercocks,
in the sway and whip of windflowers,
their pistil pages searching the spark-filled air,
fierce blooming displays.

The mediums grasp the time
turning the millennium,
find in the whisper of memory
an orienting star–
and the whisper whirls a maelstrom.

3

Someone testifies, *The coup of ages!*
Who can recall such conjuring?–
this valley remade
a measure for African winds.
The tv cameras tilt and shudder;
news reviews utterly confuse the scenery.

And her juju signs are everywhere:
sisters singing stoke and harmonize
spirited days, syncopated nights;
words of poets flash
in our faces, sounding Shu
in different rhythms–
Obatala, Shango, Ogun,

Phillis, Langston, Gwendolyn—
new lands of knowing
our commonwealth of selves,

connected souls astride
the whirlwind, swept up
to the circle of memory,
wheeling it one revolution
defined in a shift of paradigm,
and the voice from the swirl
is music to purge the stupor
of oblivion, the legacy
of thin-brewed history
we and our elders suckled,
and savored, sometimes
in soulfood pie.

4

Now she rests on a couch
in the upper room;
a mirror hangs above,
round like a halo
filled with billowing rings,
poets and seers awed
of being here,
of what they've told
and now are poised to tell,
their image of her now
a talisman, a spirit,
building with lithe love—
and their applause
is a storm of poems
rending the valley,
releasing the sound.

NOTES ON THE POETS

Elizabeth Alexander was born in New York City and raised in Washington, D.C. She has degrees from Yale University and Boston University and a Ph.D. in English from the University of Pennsylvania. Her first book of poems, *The Venus Hottentot,* was published in 1990. Her poems, short stories, and critical writings have appeared in *Paris Review, Callaloo, Village Voice,* and the *Washington Post. Diva Studies,* a full-length verse play, was produced by the Yale School of Drama in 1996. She has taught at Haverford College, the University of Chicago, the University of Pennsylvania, and Yale University. In 1999 she was the Grace Hazard Conklin Poet-in-Residence and Director of the Poetry Center at Smith College. Her most recent collections of poetry include *Antebellum Dream Book* and *Body of Life.*

Samuel Allen, born in Columbus, Ohio, has had an international career as a poet, lawyer, teacher, and translator. He was a student in James Weldon Johnson's creative writing class at Fisk University and graduated from Harvard Law School. Following military service during World War II, he studied under the G.I. Bill at the New School for Social Research and at the Sorbonne. In Paris, Richard Wright introduced him to the *Presence Africaine* circle and arranged for his first published poems to appear in that journal in 1949. Allen's interest in francophone African writers led to his translation of some of their work and of Jean-Paul Sartre's *Orphée Noir.* Allen's first collection of poetry, *Elfenbeinzähne,* was published in 1956 under the pen name Paul Vesey. He also published *Ivory Tusks and Other Poems* and *Paul Vesey's Ledger.* The most recent of his four collections, *Every Round and Other Poems,* was published by in 1987. He is the editor and one of the translators of *Poems from Africa.* He has taught at Tuskegee Institute, Wesleyan University, and Boston College.

Jabari Asim has published work in a number of anthologies and literary magazines. His poetry and fiction are included in *In the Tradition:*

An Anthology of Young Black Writers, his short story "Two Fools" appears in *Brotherman: The Odyssey of Black Men in America*; and his poems, along with the one-act play "Peace, Dog," were published in *Soulfires: Young Black Men on Love and Violence*. His poetry has been featured in *Black American Literature Forum, Obsidian II, Catalyst, Painted Bride Quarterly, Literati Internazionale, and Shooting Star Review*. A longtime critic and senior editor of *Washington Post Book World*, he has published reviews in *Salon, Los Angeles Times Book Review, Hungry Mind Review, Black Issues Book Review, Village Voice, XXL,* and *Saint Louis Post-Dispatch*.

Alvin Aubert, born in Lutcher, Louisiana, in 1930, began his teaching career at his alma mater, Southern University, Baton Rouge. He subsequently taught at the University of Oregon as Visiting Professor, at the State University of New York, Fredonia, and at Wayne State University, Detroit, where he retired as Professor Emeritus of English. While at Fredonia he founded and edited the literary journal *Obsidian* (subsequently *Obsidian II* and *Obsidian III*) and received the first of his two National Endowment for the Arts Awards for his poetry. He received the 1988 Callaloo Award from the University of Virginia for his contribution to African American cultural expression, the Spring 2000 YMCA's National Writer's Voice Award, and the Initial Xavier University of Louisiana's Activist for the Humanities Award. His *If Winter Come: Collected Poems, 1967–1994* includes new poems along with those from three earlier collections: *Against the Blues, Feeling Through,* and *South Louisiana*. His most recent collection is *Harlem Wrestler*.

Amiri Baraka, poet, activist, and playwright, was born in Newark, New Jersey, in 1934. An architect of the Black Arts movement, he has published numerous books of poetry, including *Preface to a Twenty Volume Suicide Note, The Dead Lecturer, It's Nation Time, Spirit Reach,* and *Reggae or Not*. Baraka, born LeRoi Jones, was educated at Rutgers University and Howard University. Since 1962 he has taught poetry and drama at the New School for Social Research, Columbia University, University of Buffalo, Yale University, and George Washington University. He was Professor of African Studies at the State University of New York, Stony Brook. He has also been a force in the Black Arts Repertory Theater School in Harlem and Spirit House in Newark. From 1968 to 1975 he was a founder and chair of the Congress of African People, a nationalistic Pan-African organization, and a chief organizer of the National Black Political Convention in 1972. Currently the editor of the *Black Nation,* he also edited *Cricket,* a magazine of African American music, and directed the publication of new literature through Jihad Press and Peoples War Publications.

Adisa Vera Beatty is a native of Brooklyn, New York. She received her bachelor's degree from Emerson College and joined the Dark Room Collective in 1993, while working on her M.F.A. at Brown University. Her poetry has appeared in *Callaloo, American Poetry Review, Painted Bride Quarterly,* and *Blu Magazine.* She is a human rights activist with the Malcolm X Grassroots movement and currently teaches humanities at an alternative high school in Brooklyn for juveniles coming out of prison.

Gwendolyn Brooks, known widely as the poet laureate of Illinois, was the first black writer to win a Pulitzer Prize, in 1950. Born in Topeka, Kansas, on June 7, 1917, she lived in Chicago from the age of a few weeks. A graduate of Chicago's Wilson Junior College (now Kennedy-King College), she authored more than twenty books, including *A Street in Bronzeville, Annie Allen, The Bean Eaters, In the Mecca, Maud Martha* (a novel), and two autobiographies. Among her awards and honors are her 1985 appointment to the position of Consultant in Poetry to the Library of Congress, her 1988 induction into the National Women's Hall of Fame, and the 1989 NEA Lifetime Achievement Award. In 1994 she was appointed Jefferson Lecturer by the National Endowment for the Humanities and received the National Book Awards Medal of Achievement. More awards followed, including the National Medal of Arts in 1996 and in 1997 she received the Lincoln Laureate Award, the highest award given by the state of Illinois. The recipient of over seventy honorary degrees, she taught at several colleges, including Chicago State University, where a writing center bears her name. She died on December 3, 2000, in Chicago.

Lucille Clifton was born in Depew, New York, in 1936. Her books of poetry include *Blessing the Boats: New and Selected Poems, 1988–2000,* which won the National Book Award; *The Terrible Stories,* which was nominated for the National Book Award; *The Book of Light; Quilting: Poems, 1987–1990; Next: New Poems; Good Woman: Poems and a Memoir, 1969–1980,* which was nominated for the Pulitzer Prize; *Two-Headed Woman,* also a Pulitzer Prize nominee and winner of the University of Massachusetts Press Juniper Prize; *An Ordinary Woman; Good News about the Earth;* and *Good Times.* She has also written *Generations: A Memoir* and several books for children. Her honors include an Emmy Award from the American Academy of Television Arts and Sciences, Shelley Memorial Award, and YM-YWHA Poetry Center Discovery Award. In 1999 she was elected Chancellor of the Academy of American Poets. She has served as the poet laureate of Maryland and is currently Distinguished Professor of Humanities at Saint Mary's College in Maryland.

Jayne Cortez was born in Arizona, grew up in California, and currently lives in New York City. She is the author of ten books of poems and has performed her poetry with music on nine recordings. Her poems have been translated into many languages and published in anthologies, journals, and magazines. She is the recipient of several awards, including Arts International Award, National Endowment for the Arts Award, International African Festival Award, the Langston Hughes Award, and American Book Award. Her most recent book is *Jazz Fan Looks Back,* and her most recent CD recording with her band the Firespitters is *Taking the Blues Back Home.* She directed the film *Yari Yari: Black Women Writers and the Future,* organized the international symposium "Slave Routes: The Long Memory" at New York University, and is the president of the Organization of Women Writers of Africa. She is on screen in the films *Women in Jazz* and *Poetry in Motion.*

Toi Derricotte has published three collections of poetry, *The Empress of the Death House, Natural Birth,* and *Captivity.* She received fellowships from the National Endowment for the Arts in 1985 and 1990 as well as the Lucille Medwick Memorial Award from the Poetry Society for America in 1985, a Pushcart Prize in 1989, and the Folger Shakespeare Library Poetry Book Award in 1990. Her poems have been published in a significant number of journals including *American Poetry Review, Callaloo, Iowa Review, Massachusetts Review, New England Review, Bread Loaf Quarterly,* and *Ploughshares.* She is Associate Professor of English at the University of Pittsburgh and has taught in the creative writing programs at New York University, George Mason University, Old Dominion University, and Xavier University. In 1997 Norton published her autobiography, *The Black Notebooks.* With Cornelius Eady she is cofounder of Cave Canem, a summer workshop and retreat for African American poets that began in 1996.

Joel Dias-Porter, also known as DJ Renegade, was born and raised in Pittsburgh, Pennsylvania. Formerly a professional disk jockey, he quit his job in 1991 and began living in homeless shelters, while undergoing an Africentric study program. From 1994 to 1998 he competed in the National Poetry Slam, finishing in the top five in the individual competitions, and he is the 1998 Haiku Slam Champion. His poems have been published in *Time Magazine,* the *Washington Post, Callaloo, Obsidian II, Underwood Review, Paterson Literary Review, Asheville Poetry Review, Red Brick Review,* the *GW Review,* and in the anthologies *Meow: Spoken Word from the Black Cat, 360°: A Revolution of Black Poets, Slam (The Book), Revival: Spoken Word from Lollapallooza, Poetry Nation, Beyond the Frontier, Catch a Fire,* and *The Black Rooster Social Inn: Poetry and Art of the Black Rooster Collective,* which he also edited. In 1995 he received the Furious Flower Emerging Poet Award from James Madison University. He has performed his work on the *Today Show,* in a commercial for Legal Jeans, in the documentaries *Voices against Violence,* and *SlamNation,* on BET's *Teen Summit* and *By the Book,* and in the feature film *Slam.* He is informally educated and a member of WritersCorps D.C.

Rita Dove is a former poet laureate of the United States and the youngest person ever to hold that position. She was born and raised in Akron, Ohio, and educated at Miami University and the University of Iowa. She has written several books and collections of poetry, including *Through the Ivory Gate; Fifth Sunday,* a collection of short stories; *The Yellow House on the Corner; Museum; Thomas and Beulah,* which was awarded the Pulitzer Prize in 1987; *Grace Notes; Selected Poems; The Darker Face of the Earth,* a drama in verse; and *Mother Love.* Her other honors include fellowships from the National Endowment for the Arts and the Guggenheim Foundation. Currently Commonwealth Professor of English at the University of Virginia, she lives in Charlottesville.

Cornelius Eady is the author of several books of poetry, including *Kartunes; Victims of the Latest Dance Craze,* winner of the 1985 Lamont Prize from the Academy of American Poets, *The Gathering of My Name,* nominated for the 1992 Pulitzer Prize in poetry, *You Don't Miss Your Water;* and *The Autobiography of a Jukebox.* He received a National Endowment for the Arts fellowship in literature in 1985; a John Simon Guggenheim Fellowship in poetry in 1993; a Lila Wallace-Readers Digest traveling scholarship to Tougaloo College, Mississippi, in 1992–1993; a Rockefeller Foundation fellowship to Bellagio, Italy, in 1993; and the Prairie Schooner Strousse Award in 1994. In 1999 *Running Man,* a music-theater piece he cowrote with the jazz musician Diedre Murray, was a finalist for the Pulitzer Prize in drama. He has taught poetry at SUNY, Stony Brook, where he directed its Poetry Center, and is presently Herbert Robinson Visiting Professor of Playwriting at the City College of New York. With Toi Derricotte he is cofounder of Cave Canem, a summer workshop and retreat for African American poets. In 2001 *Brutal Imagination,* his sixth book of poetry, was published. In 2002 a production of *Brutal Imagination* opened at the Vineyard Theatre, where he will spend two years working under the auspices of a TCG/Pew playwriting fellowship.

Thomas Sayers Ellis was born and raised in Washington, D.C.; studied poetry at Harvard with Seamus Heaney; cofounded the Dark Room Collective; and received an M.F.A. from Brown University in 1995. His work has appeared in *American Poetry Review; AGNI; Best American Poetry* in 1997 and 2001; *Boston Book Review; Boston Review; Callaloo; Fence; Grand Street; Hambone; Harvard Advocate; Harvard Review; Kenyon Review; Plough-*

shares; *Pushcart Prize* in 1998; *Southern Review; The Garden Thrives: Twen-tieth-Century African-American Poetry; Tin House; Giant Steps: The New Generation of African American Writers; American Poetry: The Next Generation* and *Wax Poetics*. He has received fellowships from the Ohio Arts Council; McDowell Colony; Fine Arts Work Center, Provincetown; and YADDO. In 1993 he edited *On the Verge: Emerging Poets and Artists*. He is a contributing editor of *Callaloo* and his first collection, *The Good Junk* was published in *Take Three* in 1996. He is also the author of a chapbook, *The Genuine Negro Hero,* published in 2001. He is currently Assistant Professor of English at Case Western Reserve University.

Quo Vadis Gex-Breaux lives and writes in New Orleans, Louisiana, where she also works in development for Dillard University. She has published poems in local and national journals, including *Xavier Review, New Laurel Review, Nkombo, African American Review, Black River Journal,* and the anthology *Word Up*. Her poems have also been published by *Southern Exposure* and in Spanish translation in *Quimera,* Barcelona. She also contributed to *Life Notes,* a collection of personal writing by contemporary black women, edited by Patricia Bell-Scott and published in 1994.

Nikki Giovanni entered the literary world at the height of the Black Arts movement. *Truth Is on Its Way,* a recording of her poems recited to gospel music, was one of the best-selling albums in the country in 1971. All but one of her books are still in print, with several having sold more than one hundred thousand copies. She was named Woman of the Year by three magazines, including *Ebony,* and has received of a host of honorary doctorates and awards. Her books include *Black Feeling; Black Talk/Black Judgement; My House; Ego-Tripping and Other Poems for Young People; The Women and the Men; Racism 101,* and *Love Poems,* for which she received an NAACP Image Award. A recent collection of poetry is *Blues: For All the Changes*. Giovanni is Professor of English at Virginia Polytechnic Institute and State University.

Michael S. Harper, the poet laureate of Rhode Island, is the author of eight books of poetry. He began his career with *Dear John, Dear Coltrane*. His other books include *History Is Your Own Heartbeat,* which won the Black Academy of Arts and Letters Award for poetry in 1971; *Nightmare Begins Responsibility; Images of Kin: New and Selected Poems; Images of Kin, New and Selected Poems,* which won the 1978 Melville Cane Award from the Poetry Society of America; and *Healing Songs for the Inner Ear: Poems*. He is coeditor of *Chant of Saints: A Gathering of Afro-American Literature of Art and Scholarship,* with Robert B. Stepto; and *Every Shut Eye Ain't Asleep: An Anthology of Poetry by African Americans since 1945,* with

Anthony Walton. Nominated twice for the National Book Award, he has been honored by the National Institute of Arts and Letters, National Endowment for the Arts, Guggenheim Foundation, and was elected to the American Academy of Arts and Sciences in 1995. He won the 1996 George Kent Poetry Award for *Honorable Amendments,* and in 1997 he was awarded the Claiborne Pell Award for Excellence in Arts. He is Professor of English at Brown University, where he directs the writing program.

Everett Hoagland was born and raised in Philadelphia. He graduated from Lincoln University, Pennsylvania, and Brown University. The first publications of his poetry were in Clarence Major's *The New Black Poetry* in 1968 and Dudley Randall's *The Black Poets.* Historic Broadside Press published his first collection, *Black Velvet,* in 1970. His poems have appeared in *Black World* and *First World.* More recently his poetry has appeared in *American Poetry Review, Callaloo, Crisis, Cross-Cultural Poetics, Essence, Longshot, Massachusetts Review,* and the *Progressive.* Anthologies that contain his work include *The Best American Poetry 2002, Bum Rush the Page: A Def Poetry Jam, The Body Electric, The Garden Thrives,* and *Drumvoices 2000.* His most recent book is . . . *Here* . . . *New and Selected Poems.* He was the poet laureate of New Bedford, Massachusetts, and teaches poetry workshops and African American literature at the University of Massachusetts, Dartmouth.

Major Jackson's first book of poems, *Leaving Saturn,* was selected by the poet-novelist Al Young to receive the 2000 Cave Canem Poetry Prize for the Best First Book by an African American Poet. He is the recipient of fellowships and awards from Bread Loaf Writers' Conference; Pew Fellowship in the Arts; Fine Arts Work Center, Provincetown; as well as a commission from the Chamber Orchestra of Philadelphia. His poems have appeared in *American Poetry Review, Boulevard, Callaloo, Post Road,* and the *New Yorker.* Formerly Literary Arts Curator of the Painted Bride Art Center in Philadelphia, he is Assistant Professor of English at the University of Vermont and a member of the M.F.A. Creative Writing Program at Queens College of Charlotte in North Carolina.

John Keene graduated from Harvard College and New York University, and he is a longtime member of the Dark Room Collective as well as Graduate Fellow of Cave Canem. His poetry, fiction, essays, reviews, and translations have appeared in an array of publications. He is the author of *Annotations,* and, with the artist Christopher Stackhouse, the art-text conversation *Seismosis.* His honors include the Artists' Foundation of Massachusetts and the Bread Loaf Writers' Conference. In 1997 his work was selected for *Best Gay American Fiction,* volume 2. He has received an award from the Fund for Poetry in 1999, AGNI's 2000 John

Cheever Short Fiction Prize, and the 2001 Solo Press Poetry Prize. Most recently his collection *Heroic Figures* was one of the two honorary mention finalists in the 2002 Cave Canem Poetry Prize competition. He is currently Assistant Professor of English and creative writing at Northwestern University.

Dolores Kendrick, the poet laureate of Washington, D.C., is the author of three books of poetry: *Through the Ceiling, Now is the Thing to Praise,* and *The Women of Plums: Poems in the Voices of Slave Women.* She is the recipient of the Anisfield-Wolf Award, New York Public Library's Best Book for Teenagers Award for *The Women of Plums,* a Fulbright, and a National Endowment for the Arts Award. Her stage adaptation of *The Women of Plums* won the New York Playwrights Award in 1997 and was produced at the Kennedy Center in 1997–1998. Another production was presented at the Karamu Theatre in Cleveland, Ohio. Her work has appeared in *Beloit Poetry Journal, Ms. Magazine,* and in magazines in China and Japan. She is also the recipient of the George Kent Award for Literature, given by the Gwendolyn Brooks Foundation of Chicago University. She has read in the Gertrude Whittal Series of the Library of Congress, among other places, and is Vira I. Heinz Professor Emerita at Phillips Exeter Academy.

Yusef Komunyakaa was born in Bogalusa, Louisiana, in 1947. His books of poetry include *Pleasure Dome: New and Collected Poems, 1975–1999; Talking Dirty to the Gods; Thieves of Paradise,* which was a finalist for the National Book Critics Circle Award; *Neon Vernacular: New and Selected Poems, 1977–1989,* for which he received the Pulitzer Prize and the Kingsley Tufts Poetry Award; *Magic City; Dien Cai Dau,* which won the Dark Room Poetry Prize; *I Apologize for the Eyes in My Head,* winner of the San Francisco Poetry Center Award; and *Copacetic.* He is coeditor of *The Jazz Poetry Anthology,* with J. A. Sascha Feinstein; and, with Martha Collins, cotranslator of *The Insomnia of Fire* by Nguyen Quang Thieu. His honors include the William Faulkner Prize from the Université de Rennes; Thomas Forcade Award; Hanes Poetry Prize; fellowships from the Fine Arts Work Center, Provincetown; Lousiana Arts Council; and the Bronze Star for service in Vietnam, where he served as correspondent and managing editor of *Southern Cross.* In 1999 he was elected Chancellor of the Academy of American Poets.

Pinkie Gordon Lane is a native of Philadelphia, Pennsylvania, who has lived in Louisiana for over forty years. She was the first African American woman to earn a Ph.D. from Louisiana State University, at a time when that institution was emerging from segregated enrollment. She also became the first African American to serve as state poet laureate, serving from 1989 to 1992. She is the author of five books of poems, including *Elegy for Etheridge*. Her work has appeared in a number of anthologies and literary magazines, some while she was Professor of English and Chair of the Department of English at Southern University in Baton Rouge, Louisiana. Honors for her work include recognition from Amistad Research Center, New Orleans; Delta Sigma Theta Sorority; the College Language Association; National Council of Teachers of English; Furious Flower Poetry Conference, James Madison University; and an honorary doctorate degree from Spelman College, her undergraduate alma mater.

Naomi Long Madgett's career as poet spans six decades. She is the author of eight collections of poetry, including *Octavia and Other Poems* and *Remembrances of Spring: Collected Early Poems*. A documentary film based on *Octavia* won the Golden Apple Award for Excellence from the National Education Media Network. She is also the editor of two anthologies, including *Adam of Ifè: Black Women in Praise of Black Men*. Her poems have appeared in numerous journals, anthologies, and textbooks. The poet laureate of Detroit since 2001, her awards include American Book Award, Michigan Artist Award, induction into the Michigan Women's Hall of Fame, and honorary degrees. She is Professor Emerita of English at Eastern Michigan University, and since 1972 she has been publisher and editor of Lotus Press, sponsor of the annual Naomi Long Madgett Poetry Award for an outstanding script by an African American.

Haki R. Madhubuti serves, as a poet, publisher, editor, and educator, as a pivotal figure in the development of a strong black literary tradition. He has published twenty-two books, some under his former name Don L. Lee, and is one of the world's best-selling authors of poetry and nonfiction, with books in print in excess of three million. His *Black Men: Obsolete, Single, Dangerous? The African American Family in Transition* has sold over one million copies since its 1990 publication. He is the author of *Claiming Earth: Race, Rage, Rape, Redemption; Ground Work: New and Selected Poems 1966–1996; HeartLove: Wedding and Love Poems;* and the coeditor of *Releasing the Spirit: A Collection of Literary Works from Gallery 37.* A proponent of independent black institutions, he is the founder, publisher, and chair of the board of Third World Press; cofounder of the Institute of Positive Education at the New Concept School; and cofounder of Betty Shabazz International Charter School in Chicago, Illinois. An award-winning poet and recipient of honors that include recognition from National Endowment for the Arts, National Endowment for the Humanities fellowships, and Illinois Arts Council Award, he is Professor of English and founder and Director Emeritus of the Gwendolyn Brooks Center, Chicago State University.

Garrett McDowell was born in Oklahoma, grew up in California, and now lives and writes in Washington, D.C. He has won a Larry Neal Award for fiction and is a founding member of the Writers' Workshop of the African American Writers Guild. Among his publications are short fiction in *Streetlights* and essays in *Encyclopedia of African-American Education, LaDocumentation Francaise,* and *Asian Survey.*

Adam David Miller has for four decades supported and participated in the community of black arts and letters. He has written articles and reviews on the black aesthetic, the teaching of black literature, blaxploitation films, black theatre, black dance, and the works of black poets and writers. His anthology *Dices or Black Bones,* containing work by then little-known poets Lucille Clifton and Al Young, won the California Association of Teachers Award in 1970. *Forever Afternoon,* his second of five books of verse, won the Naomi Long Madgett Poetry Award in 1994. He has been awarded other prizes, including a National Endowment for the Humanities Fellowship for study in West Africa.

E. Ethelbert Miller has been Director of the African American Resource Center at Howard University since 1974. He is the editor of *In Search of Color Everywhere,* which was awarded the 1994 PEN Oakland Josephine Miles Award. The anthology was also a Book of the Month Club selection. He has served as Visiting Professor at the University of Nevada, Las Vegas, and at Central Michigan University. In 1996 he was the Jessie Ball DuPont Scholar at Emory and Henry College and was awarded the 1995 O. B. Hardison Jr. Poetry Prize. In 1997 he was presented with the Stephen Henderson Poetry Award by the African American Literature and Culture Society. He received an honorary doctorate of literature from Emory and Henry College in 1996. His collections of poetry include *Whispers, Secrets, and Promises, Buddha Weeping in Winter,* and *Beyond the Frontier.* His memoir, *Fathering Words: The Making of an African American Writer,* was published in 2000.

Lenard D. Moore was educated at Shaw University and North Carolina A&T State University. He is founder and Executive Director of the Carolina African American Writers' Collective and cofounder of the Washington Street Writers Group. His poems, essays, and reviews have appeared in numerous languages and publications around the world. His poetry has appeared in over forty anthologies, most recently in *Fives: Fifty Poems by Serbian and American Poets, Beyond the Frontier: African-American Poetry for the Twenty-first Century, The Haiku Anthology, Trouble the*

Water: Two Hundred and Fifty Years of African American Poetry, and *The Garden Thrives: Twentieth Century African American Poetry.* He is the author of *The Open Eye; Forever Home;* and *Desert Storm: A Brief History.* His awards include the Haiku Museum of Tokyo Award in 1983 and 1994, Indies Arts Award in 1996, Margaret Walker Creative Writing Award in 1997, Tar Heel of the Week Award in 1998, and the Alumni Achievement Award University in 2000 from Shaw University. He has been Cave Canem Fellow (1998–2000) and serves on the North Carolina Literary Hall of Fame Committee. He has served as a judge for the Furious Flower Poetry Prize.

Opal Moore, Associate Professor of English teaching fiction, poetry writing, and African American literature, serves as Chair of the Department of English at Spelman College, Atlanta. A native Chicagoan, she completed her B.F.A. at Illinois Wesleyan University and an M.A. in drawing and an M.F.A. in the Fiction Writing (English) from Iowa Writer's Workshop. She was a Fulbright scholar to Germany in 1994 and a Dupont scholar at Hollins University. Her fiction and poetry have appeared in literary journals and anthologies, including *Callaloo, Connecticut Review, Honey, Hush! An Anthology of African American Women's Humor,* and *Homeplaces: Stories of the Women Writers.* Her collection of poems *Lot's Daughters* is forthcoming from Third World Press. She also created a suite of poems, "The Children of Middle Passage," for *The Delfina Project,* a collaborative performance artwork inspired by the images of the contemporary artist Arturo Lindsay.

Raymond R. Patterson was born in Harlem, New York, and educated at Lincoln University, Pennsylvania, and New York University. He was the author of *26 Ways of Looking at a Black Man and Other Poems* and *Elemental Blues,* as well as an unpublished book-length poem on the life of Phillis Wheatley, and two opera librettos, *David Walker* and *Goree.* His poetry has appeared in the *Transatlantic Review, Ohio Review, Crisis, Beloit Poetry Journal, Drumvoices Revue,* and *ELF.* His work is also included in the anthologies *The Poetry of the Negro, New Black Voices, Soulscript, Norton Introduction to Literature, A Geography of Poets,* and, more recently, *Every Shut Eye Ain't Asleep, The Second Set: The Jazz Poetry Anthology, Trouble the Water: Two Hundred and Fifty Years of African-American Poetry, I Feel a Little Jumpy around You,* and *The Best American Poetry of 1996.* He taught at the City College of the City University of New York, where he cofounded and directed the annual Langston Hughes Festival from 1973 to 1993. He died in 2001.

Sterling D. Plumpp was born in Clinton, Mississippi, on January 30, 1940. As a boy he was raised by his maternal grandparents, who were sharecroppers. Plumpp never attended school a full year. At the age of fifteen, he moved to Jackson, Mississippi, where he completed elementary and high school and graduated as class valedictorian in 1960. He spent two years at Saint Benedict's College and later joined the army. In the 1960s he moved to Chicago and worked at the main post office. Currently he is Professor of English and African American Studies at the University of Illinois, Chicago. During his tenure at the University of Illinois, he has won two Amoco-Silver Circle Awards for excellence in teaching. He also won the Carl Sandburg Literary Prize for poetry in 1983 for *The Mojo Hands Call, I Must Go.* He has written numerous books, including *Hornam; Harriet Tubman,* which is autobiographical; *Ornate with Smoke, Blues: The Story Always Untold;* and *Half Black, Half Blacker.*

Bernice Johnson Reagon is a composer, song leader, historian, and curator. She was born in 1942 in Albany, Georgia, and earned her undergraduate degree at Spelman College. In 1975 she received a Ph.D. from Howard University. As a composer and song leader in the nineteenth-century Southwest Georgia choral tradition, she founded Sweet Honey in the Rock in 1973. As a historian and scholar, she is Distinguished Professor of History at the American University and Curator Emerita at the Smithsonian Institution, National Museum of American History. Author of several publications, she has served as a consultant, composer, and performer in many films, two of which were award-winning programs on PBS, *Eyes on the Prize* and *We Shall Overcome.* She received a MacArthur Fellowship in 1989, was awarded the Presidential Medal, and earned the Charles Frankel Prize for outstanding contribution to a public understanding of the humanities in 1995. She received an Isadora Duncan Award for the score to *Rock,* directed by Alonzo King for LINES Contemporary Ballet Company, in 1996.

Eugene B. Redmond, the poet laureate of East Saint Louis, Illinois, and author of *Drumvoices: The Mission of Afro-American Poetry,* has been published in hundreds of anthologies and journals, including *Black Orpheus, Essence, Cavalcade, Giant Talk: Anthology of Third World Writings, The Furious Flowering of African American Poetry, Bum Rush the Page: A Def Poetry Jam, Black American Literature Forum, Miles Davis and American Culture, Saint Louis Muse, Black Scholar, Saint Louis Post-Dispatch, The Oxford Anthology of African American Poetry,* the *East Saint Louis Monitor, Understanding the New Black Poetry, Multicultural Review, Eyeball, Confrontation,* and *River of Song.* Winner of an American Book Award for *The Eye in the Ceiling,* he has also won a National Endowment for the Arts Creative Writing Fellowship; Outstanding Faculty Research Award, California State, Sacramento; Pushcart Prize; Tribute to an Elder Award from African Poetry

Theater; and First Prize in Washington University's Annual Festival of the Arts Poetry Contest. In 1999 he was inducted into the National Hall of Fame for Writers of African Descent, Gwendolyn Brooks Center, Chicago State University. The Eugene B. Redmond Writers Club, founded in 1986, copublishes *Drumvoices Revue* with Southern Illinois University, Edwardsville, where he is founding editor of the journal, Professor of English, and Chair of the Creative Writing Committee.

Dorothy Marie Rice is a teacher, writer, poet, and artist. She has published poetry in several magazines, including *Obsidian II: Black Literature in Review*. She was one of three finalists in the Furious Flower poetry competition and the winner of several Irene Leache literary competitions. She coauthored two books with her cousin Muriel M. Branch about the life of Maggie L. Walker: *Miss Maggie* and *Pennies to Dollars*. With her mother, Lucille Mabel Walthall Payne, she coauthored *The Seventeenth Child*. She continues to write and present her poems to schools, churches, and community groups. She is a resource teacher for literature and history in public schools in Richmond, Virginia.

Kalamu ya Salaam is a New Orleans, Louisiana, editor, writer, filmmaker, and founder of Nommo Literary Society, a black writers workshop; cofounder of Runagate Multimedia publishing company; leader of the WordBand, a poetry performance ensemble; and moderator of e-Drum, a listserv for writers and supporters of black literature. His most recent book is the anthology *360°: A Revolution of Black Poets. The Magic of Juju: An Appreciation of the Black Arts Movement* is forthcoming. His most recent spoken-word CD is *My Story, My Song*. For thirteen years he was editor of *The Black Collegian* and for five years a member of the Free Southern Theater.

Mona Lisa Saloy received an M.F.A. at Louisiana State University, Baton Rouge; an M.A. in creative writing at San Francisco State University; and a B.A. at the University of Washington, Seattle. She is the author of *Between Laughter and Tears: Black Mona Lisa Poems,* a chapbook. Her most recent work appears in *Double Dealer Redux, From a Bend in the River: One Hundred New Orleans Poets, Ishmael Reed's Konch,* and *My Mother Had a Dream: African-American Women Share Their Mother's Words of Wisdom.* Some of her poems appear in *Immortelles, Poems of Life and Death by New Southern Writers* and the *Southern Review.* She is featured in the 1994 video anthology from the American Poetry Archives entitled *Color: A Sampling of Contemporary African American Writers.* Other published poems appear in *Word Up, Black Poetry of the Eighties from the Deep South, Black Scholar,* the *Haight Ashberry Literary Journal, Dark Waters, Testimony,* and *Louisiana Laurels.* At Dillard University she has been Director of Creative Writing for the past four years and is currently Assistant Professor of English and a doctoral candidate in American literature at Louisiana State University.

Sonia Sanchez is the author of numerous books, including *Homecoming, We a BaddDDD People, Love Poems, I've Been a Woman: New and Selected Poems, Sound Investment and Other Stories, Homegirls and Handgrenades, Under a Soprano Sky, Wounded in the House of a Friend,* and *Like the Singing Coming off the Drums.* In addition to being a contributing editor to *Black Scholar* and the *Journal of African Studies,* she has edited two anthologies: *We Be Word Sorcerers: Twenty-Five Stories by Black Americans* and *360° of Blackness Coming at You.* She is a recipient of the National Endowment for the Arts Award, Lucretia Mott Award in 1984, Outstanding Arts Award from the Pennsylvania Coalition of One Hundred Black Women, and the Community Service Award from the National Black Caucus of State Legislators. She is a winner of the 1985 American Book Award for her *Homegirls and Handgrenades,* Governor's Award for Excellence in Humanities in 1988, Peace and Freedom Award in 1989 from the Women's International League for Peace and Freedom, and a Pew Fellowship in the Arts in 1992–1993. She has shared her poetry throughout the United States as well as abroad, and her work is studied in *BMA: The Sonia Sanchez Literary Review.* She was Laura Carnell Chair of English and Chair of the Women's Studies Program at Temple University until her retirement in 2001.

Lamont B. Steptoe is an award-winning poet, born and raised in Pittsburgh, Pennsylvania. He is the author of nine books of poetry, including *Crimson River, American Morning/Mourning, Mad Minute, Catfish and Neckbone Jazz, Dusty Road, Uncle's South China Sea Blue Nightmare,* and *In the Kitchens of the Masters.* He has been nominated twice for a Pushcart Prize in poetry; he was a 1996 recipient of Pennsylvania Council on the Arts Fellowship in poetry; and the Kuntu Writers Workshop of Pittsburgh, Pennsylvania, honored him with a Lifetime Achievement Award in poetry. He is a photographer and publisher-founder of Whirlwind Press and a Vietnam veteran. His work has appeared in numerous journals, including the *Painted Bride Quarterly, Longshot Review, Tribes Magazine, Konch, Drumvoices Revue, Rattapallax, Negative Capability, Asphodel, Seven Arts Magazine, Mickle Street Review, Half Dozen of the Other, Heart Quarterly, Lips, BMA: The Sonia Sanchez Literary Review,* and *Medicinal Purposes.* His poetry and photography regularly appear in the *REAL NEWS,* a black progressive newspaper in Philadelphia.

Sharan Strange grew up in Orangeburg, South Carolina, was educated at Radcliffe College, and received an M.F.A. in poetry from Sarah Lawrence College. Her poems have appeared in several journals and anthologies, in museum exhibitions in New York and Boston, and on CD recordings. Her collection *Ash* won the 2000 Barnard New Women Poets Prize. She was a founding member of the Dark Room Collective and an original curator and host of the Dark Room Reading Series. She is a contributing and advisory editor of *Callaloo* and currently teaches English at Spelman College.

Lorenzo Thomas was born in the Republic of Panama; graduated from Queens College, New York City; and served in Vietnam. He began his literary career as part of the Black Arts movement and was included in the seminal *Black Fire* poetry anthology edited by Amiri Baraka. He has worked with Poetry-in-the-Schools Programs throughout the United States. As a music historian he has written articles and books on the blues. His poetry collections are *A Visible Island, Fit Music, Dracula, Framing the Sunrise, Chances Are Few,* and *The Bathers.* His poetry has been published in a number of anthologies, including *Texas Stories and Poems, Liquid City,* and *New Black Voices.* His work has appeared in many journals, including *African American Review; Arrowsmith; Blues Unlimited* (England); *Living Blues; Subdream* (Austria); *Ploughshares;* and *Popular Music and Society.* He has contributed articles to the *African American Encyclopedia, Oxford Companion to African American Literature,* and *American Literary Scholarship.* A new collection entitled *Es Gibt Zeugen* has recently been published in Germany. Associate Professor of English at the University of Houston, Downtown, he teaches American literature and creative writing.

Askia M. Touré is one of the architects of both the Black Arts and African-centered black studies movements as well as a pioneer in the black aesthetic. A political activist, he served with the Student National Co-ordinating Committee's Atlantic Project. An internationally published poet, he is featured in a host of anthologies and is the author of five books, including the epic novel-in-verse *From the Pyramids to the Projects,* winner of the 1989 American Book Award for literature. In 1995 he was awarded the Gwendolyn Brooks Lifetime Achievement Award from the Gwendolyn Brooks Center, Chicago State University. His most recent volume, *Dawn Song! The Epic Memory of Askia Touré* was published in 2000. Recently he was Artist-in-Residence at Ogunnaike Galleria, a cultural institution and cafe, Boston, Massachusetts.

Natasha Trethewey is the author of *Domestic Work,* which won the 2001 Lillian Smith Book Award, and *Bellocq's Ophelia.* She is the recipient of fellowships from the National Endowment for the Arts, Alabama

State Council on the Arts, and the Bunting Fellowship Program of the Radcliffe Institute for Advanced Studies at Harvard University. Currently she is Assistant Professor of English at Emory University.

Jerry W. Ward Jr. is Professor of English and African world studies at Dillard University. From 1970 to 2002 he taught at Tougaloo College, Mississippi, and was Lawrence Durgin Professor of Literature. He is the compiler and editor of *Trouble the Water: Two Hundred and Fifty Years of African American Poetry* and has published poems and critical essays in a number of journals and anthologies. He is one of the founders of the Richard Wright Circle.

Carole B. Weatherford's poetry is collected in the prize-winning chapbook *The Tan Chanteuse* and in *The Tarbaby on the Soapbox,* a chapbook forthcoming from Long Leaf Press. She is coauthor of *Somebody's Knocking at Your Door: AIDS and the African-American Church,* and she has written several children's books, including *Sink or Swim: African-American Lifesavers of the Outer Banks* and *Juneteenth Jamboree.* Recipient of a North Carolina Arts Council Fellowship and the Furious Flower Poetry Prize, she resides in High Point, North Carolina.

Afaa Michael Weaver, a playwright, fiction writer, and freelance journalist, was born in Baltimore, Maryland, in 1951. His recent collections of poetry include *Multitudes: Poems Selected and New, The Lights of God,* and *Talisman.* Under the name Michael S. Weaver, he published *Timber and Prayer: The Indian Pond Poems, My Father's Geography,* and *Water Song.* He has received fellowships from the National Endowment for the Arts and Pennsylvania Council on the Arts. Currently he is the editor of *Obsidian II* and is Alumnae Professor of English at Simmons College in Boston.

Kevin Young's first book, *Most Way Home,* was selected for the National Poetry Series and won the Zacharis First Book Award from *Ploughshares.* His second book of poems, *To Repel Ghosts,* is based on the work of the late artist Jean-Michel Basquiat and a finalist for the James McLaughlin Prize from the Academy of American Poets. His most recent book of poems is *Jelly Roll: A Blues.* His poetry and essays have appeared in the *New Yorker, Paris Review, Kenyon Review, Paideuma,* and *Callaloo* and have been featured on National Public Radio's *All Things Considered.* He is the editor of *Giant Steps: The New Generation of African American Writers* and the anthology *Blues Poems.* A former Stegner Fellow in Poetry at Stanford University, he is currently Ruth Lilly Professor of Poetry at Indiana University.

ACKNOWLEDGMENTS

Elizabeth Alexander: "The Josephine Baker Museum," "At the Beach," and "Passage" from *Body of Life,* Copyright © 1996, published by Tia Chucha Press. Reprinted by permission of the author.

Samuel Allen: "The Apple Trees in Sussex" from *Every Round and Other Poems,* copyright © 1987, published by Lotus Press. "A Moment, Please," "The Lingering Doubt," and "To Satch" copyright © by Samuel Allen. Reprinted by permission of the author.

Jabari Asim: "1st Lt. Vernon J. Baker: Hero on the Hill (Company C, 370th Infantry Regiment, 92nd Division)," "Let's Just Tell It," and "Baby's Breath" reprinted by permission of the author.

Alvin Aubert: "Nat Turner in the Clearing," "James Baldwin, 1924–1987," and "December 1982/Detroit" reprinted by permission of the author.

Amiri Baraka: "I Am" and "In the Funk World" from *Funklore,* Copyright © 1998, published by Cultural. Reprinted by permission of the author. "John Coltrane (1926–1967)" from *Eulogies,* copyright © 1997, published by Marsilio. Reprinted by permission of the author.

Adisa Vera Beatty: "Distance," "Memorization," and "Geography" reprinted by permission of the author.

Gwendolyn Brooks: "The Second Sermon on the Warpland" from *Blacks,* copyright © 1991 by The David Company, Chicago. Reprinted by permission of Brooks Permissions. "Winnie" copyright © 1988, 1991 by Third World Press. Reprinted by permission of Brooks Permissions. "A Bronzeville Mother Loiters in Mississippi. Meanwhile, a Mississippi Mother Burns Bacon" from *Blacks,* copyright © 1987 by Third World Press. Reprinted by permission of Brooks Permissions. "We Real Cool" and "The Near-Johannesburg Boy" from *Blacks* by The David Company, Chicago. Reprinted by permission of Brooks Permissions. "Uncle Seagram" from *Children Coming Home,* copyright © 1991 by The David Company, Chicago.

Lucille Clifton: "dialysis," "donor," and "1994" from *Blessing the Boats: New and Selected Poems 1988-2000."* Copyright © 2000 by Lucille Clifton. Reprinted with the permission of BOA Editions, Ltd.

Jayne Cortez: "There It Is," "The Guitars I Used to Know," and "The Heavy Headed Dance" reprinted by permission of the author.

Toi Derricotte: "The Minks" from *Captivity,* published by University of Pittsburgh Press. Reprinted by permission of the author. "After a Reading at a Black College" and "For Black Women Who Are Afraid," from *Tender.* Copyright © 1997. Reprinted by permission of the author.

Joel Dias-Porter (DJ Renegade): "Fireflies in a Jar," "Thursday Poem," and "Subterranean Night-Colored Magus" reprinted by permission of the author.

Rita Dove: "Freedom Ride," "Claudette Colvin Goes to Work," "Rosa," and "The Enactment" from *On the Bus with Rosa Parks*. Copyright 1999 by Rita Dove. Used by permission of W. W. Norton & Company, Inc.

Cornelius Eady: "How I Got Born," "Composite," and "Birthing" copyright © 2001 by Cornelius Eady. Reprinted by permission of the author.

Thomas Sayers Ellis: "Sir Nose D'VoidofFunk" and "View of the Library of Congress from Paul Laurence Dunbar High School" reprinted by permission of the author.

Quo Vadis Gex-Breaux: "Jazz Rain," "Padded Steps/Sister Song (a litany)," "Wisdom Is," and "Memory Waves" reprinted by permission of the author.

Nikki Giovanni: "The Wrong Kitchen" from *Blues: For All the Changes,* copyright © 1999. Reprinted by permission of the author. "Legacies" copyright © 1970 and "Nikki-Rosa" copyright © 1968, from *The Selected Poems of Nikki Giovanni*. Reprinted by permission of the author.

Michael S. Harper: "Dear John, Dear Coltrane," "Last Affair: Bessie's Blues Song," and "High Modes: Vision as Ritual: Confirmation" reprinted by permission of the author.

Everett Hoagland: "From Ground Zero," from *Sunday Standard* Times, copyright © 2001 Everett Hoagland. "How Could All That Have Happened Here?" copyright © 2001 Everett Hoagland. "Time Break," copyright © 1998 Everett Hoagland. Reprinted by permission of the author.

Major Jackson: "Indian Song," "Block Party," "To Afaa Michael S. Weaver," and "Some Kind of Crazy" reprinted by permission of the author.

John Keene: "After C (3): Tayloriana" and "The Haymarket" copyright © 2002 John Keene. Reprinted by permission of the author.

Dolores Kendrick: "For Gwendolyn Brooks: As I Civilize a Space" and "Where the Grieved Ones Sat" copyright © 1997 Dolores Kendrick. "The Drowned River" copyright © 1996 Dolores Kendrick. Reprinted by permission of the author.

Yusef Komunyakaa: "Songs for My Father" from *Neon Vernacular* (Wesleyan). Reprinted by permission of the author.

Pinkie Gordon Lane: "Girl at the Window" copyright © 1991 Pinkie Gordon Lane. "Lyric: I Am Looking at Music" and "Children" copyright © Pinkie Gordon Lane. Reprinted by permission of the author.

Naomi Long Madgett: "Reluctant Light" copyright © 1993 Naomi Long Madgett. "The Last Happy Day" from *Octavia and Other Poems,* published by Third World Press, copyright © 1988. Reprinted by permission of the author. "Packrat" from *Exits and Entrances,* copyright © 1978. Reprinted by permission of the author.

Haki R. Madhubuti: "Books as Answer" and "The B Network" from *HeartLove: Wedding & Love Poems,* published by Third World Press, copyright © 1998 Haki R. Madhubuti. Reprinted by permission of the author. "Mothers" from *Groundwork: New and Selected Poems,* published by Third World Press, copyright © 1996 Haki Madhubuti. Reprinted by permission of the author.

Garrett McDowell: "A Blooming in the Valley" copyright © 1994 Garret McDowell. Reprinted by permission of the author.

Adam David Miller: "My Trip," "Forever Afternoon," and "Song of the Wheel" reprinted by permission of the author.

E. Ethelbert Miller: "Roy Campanella: January, 1958," "Bringing Back the Draft," and "Whispers, Secrets, and Promises" from *Whispers, Secrets and Promises,* published by Black Classic Press, copyright © 1998 E. Ethelbert Miller. Reprinted by permission of the author.

Lenard D. Moore: "Airport" and "Black Girl Tap Dancing" reprinted by permission of the author.

Opal Moore: "Eulogy for Sister" from *Callaloo,* published by John Hopkins Press, copyright © 1996 Opal Moore and reprinted by permission of the author. "The Taste of Life Going On" reprinted by permission of the author.

Raymond R. Patterson: "Harlem Suite" from *Drumvoices Revue*, Fall–Winter 1994–95, vol. 4, nos. 1 and 2. Copyright © Raymond Patterson and reprinted by permission of the author. "Forerunner" reprinted by permission of the author. "Baobab" from *Say That the River Turns: The Impact of Gwendolyn Brooks*, published by Third World Press, copyright © 1987 Raymond Patterson. Reprinted by permission of the author.

Sterling D. Plumpp: "Be-Bop" from *Hornman*, published by Third World Press, copyright © 1995 Sterling D. Plumpp. "History, Hollers, and Horn" and "Ornate with Smoke" from *Ornate with Smoke*, published by Third World Press, copyright © 1997 Sterling D. Plumpp. "Mary" from *Blues Narratives*, published by Tia Chucha Press, 1999. Reprinted by permission of the author.

Bernice Johnson Reagon: "Greed" copyright © 1994 Bernice Johnson Reagon. "They Are All Falling around Me" copyright © 1975 Bernice Johnson Reagon. Reprinted by permission of the author.

Eugene B. Redmond: "New York Seizures" from *The Eye in the Ceiling: Selected Poems of Eugene B. Redmond*, published by Harlem River Press, copyright © 1991 Eugene B. Redmond and reprinted by permission of the author. "11-haiku-poem for a magnificent million" revised 1999 and reprinted by permission of the author.

Dorothy Marie Rice: "Taproots," "Ambrosia," and "Remains" reprinted by permission of the author.

Kalamu ya Salaam: "Sharing is hereditary," "The Call of the Wild," and "Directions for Understanding Modern Jazz Criticism" reprinted by permission of the author.

Mona Lisa Saloy: "The 'N' Word" copyright © 2001 Mona Lisa Saloy. "This Poem Is for You, My Sister" and "We've Come This Far" from *Between Laughter and Tears: Black Mona Lisa Poems*, published by Black Bayou Press, copyright © 1995 Mona Lisa Saloy. Reprinted by permission of the author.

Sonia Sanchez: "Ballad" and "Letter to Ezekiel Mphahlele" from *Homegirls & Handgrenades*, published by Thunder's Mouth Press, copyright © 1984 Sonia Sanchez. "Under a Soprano Sky" and "Philadelphia: Spring, 1985" from *Under a Soprano Sky*, published by African World Press, copyright © 1987 Sonia Sanchez. "For Sweet Honey in the Rock" from *Shake Loose My Skin*, published by Beacon Press, copyright © 1999 Sonia Sanchez. "For Sister Gwen Brooks" from *Like the Singing Coming off the Drums*, published by Beacon Press, copyright © 1998 Sonia Sanchez. Reprinted by permission of the author.

Lamont B. Steptoe: "Spookism," "Contraband," and "Coming Ashore" published by Whirlwind Press, copyright © 1997 Lamont B. Steptoe. Reprinted by permission of the author.

Sharan Strange: "Night Work" from *American Poetry Review*, copyright © Sharan Strange, reprinted by permission of the author. "Hunger" and "Offering" from *Callaloo*, vol. 16, no. 1, reprinted by permission of Johns Hopkins University Press.

Lorenzo Thomas: "Dangerous Doubts" and "L'Argent" copyright © 1996 Lorenzo Thomas. "Back in the Day" copyright © 1995 Lorenzo Thomas. Reprinted by permission of the author.

Askia M. Touré: "Summer Worlds: A Mythic Landscape," "Ab*original* Elegy: The Once and Future Queen," and "O Lord of Light! A Mystic Sage Returns to Realms of Eternity" reprinted by permission of the author.

Natasha Trethewey: "Limen" from *New England Review*, copyright © 1999 Natasha Trethewey. "Bellocq's Ophelia" from *Southern Review*, copyright © 1998 Natasha Trethewey. "Drapery Factory, Gulfport, Mississippi, 1956" from *Agni Review*, copyright © Natasha Trethewey. Reprinted by permission of the author.

Jerry Ward Jr.: "I Have Felt the Gulf: Mississippi," "Journey 55," and "After the Report from Iron Mountain" reprinted by permission of the author.

Carole B. Weatherford: "The Tan Chanteuse" from *The Tan Chanteuse* and *Callaloo*, copyright © Carole B. Weatherford. "From Birmingham to Bristol in a Boxcar" from *The*